D1012951

GO DIRECTLY TO JAIL

GO DIRECTLY TO JAIL

THE CRIMINALIZATION OF ALMOST EVERYTHING

•

Edited by
GENE HEALY

CATO INSTITUTE
Washington, D.C.

Copyright © 2004 by Cato Institute.
All rights reserved.
Second Printing: December 2004

Library of Congress Cataloging-in-Publication Data

Go directly to jail : the criminalization of almost everything /
    edited by Gene Healy.
    p. cm.
Includes bibliographical references and index.
ISBN 1-930865-63-5 (alk. paper)
    1. Criminal law—United States.   2. White collar crime—United
States.   I. Healy, Gene, 1970—   II. Title.

KF9223.G57 2004
346.7304'8—dc22

                                                            2004058470

Cover design by Parker Wallman.

Printed in the United States of America.

CATO INSTITUTE
1000 Massachusetts Ave., N.W.
Washington, D.C. 20001
www.cato.org

Contents

Introduction

Gene Healy

The criminal law is a powerful weapon: In the right hands, wielded for the right ends, it is an indispensable instrument of justice. In the wrong hands, wielded indiscriminately, it can become an agent of appalling injustice.

For that reason, the legal reformers of America's founding generation reserved the criminal sanction mainly for serious, morally culpable offenses. In his *History of American Law*, Lawrence Friedman notes that the American Revolutionaries "identified oppression with abuse of criminal law, and identified the rights of man with basic rights to fair criminal trial." To prevent abuse, the newly independent United States "shrank the concept of state crime to an almost irreducible minimum. The men who drafted penal codes were willing to accept a lot of slippage in enforcement to protect the innocent, and (even more) to keep the government in check."[1]

That no longer holds. As the American Bar Association's Task Force on the Federalization of Crime put it in 1998, "So large is the present body of federal criminal law that there is no conveniently accessible, complete list of federal crimes."[2] There are now more than 4,000 federal crimes, an increase of one-third since 1980.[3] Many of those crimes, spread out through some 27,000 pages of the U.S. Code, incorporate violations of federal regulations that are in turn spread throughout the tens of thousands of pages of the *Code of Federal Regulations*. As a result, even teams of legal researchers— let alone ordinary citizens—cannot reliably ascertain what federal law prohibits.[4]

As federal criminal law has metastasized, federal criminal sanctions have become more indiscriminate. At one time, the common law doctrines of *mens rea* ("guilty mind") and *actus reus* ("guilty act") cabined the reach of criminal sanctions, but those protections have eroded dramatically in the past 50 years. Today it's possible to send a person to prison without showing criminal intent or even a culpable act—as when business owners and corporate executives are convicted under the "responsible corporate officer doctrine" for negligent failure to supervise the acts of their employees.[5]

Increasingly, legislators are coming to view the criminal sanction as merely another item in their regulatory toolkit. Want to show you're serious about a given social problem, whether it's pollution, corporate malfeasance, or e-mail spam? Make it a crime. In some cases, the criminal law gets invoked for matters more properly handled through civil lawsuits. In others, political actors use it to criminalize behavior that shouldn't be the subject of any legal sanction at all. As a result, the criminal law is becoming unmoored from its ethical foundations.

At the same time, America's criminal justice system is becoming ever more centralized and punitive because of rampant federalization and mandatory minimum sentencing. The result is a labyrinthine criminal code, a burgeoning prison population, and a system that would scarcely be recognizable to the Founders.[6]

Examples of overcriminalization are legion. Under the McCain-Feingold campaign finance law passed in 2002, unions and corporations—as well as their officers—now face severe criminal penalties for broadcasting advocacy messages that "refe[r] to a clearly identified candidate" in the run-up to an election.[7] The Sarbanes-Oxley Act of 2002 imposes criminal penalties, including prison sentences, for executives who certify financial statements that prove incorrect. And the War on Drugs grows ever more draconian: the federal government continues to open new fronts in the battle against drug use, as if federal resources were limitless and there were no genuine terrorist threats on the horizon. The Bush administration has begun cracking down on pain-management doctors for alleged prescription drug abuse, sending a message to other doctors to err on the side of underprescribing for patients in pain.[8] Comedian Tommy Chong was sentenced on September 11, 2003, to nine months in jail for selling water pipes and other drug paraphernalia on the Internet.[9]

At times, the trend toward overcriminalization can take a comical turn, as evidenced by what might be termed the "criminalization of bad taste." In May 2004, the Louisiana House Criminal Justice Committee approved a bill that would penalize the unfortunate tendency of America's youth to adopt a sartorial trend commonly associated with plumbers: "It shall be unlawful for any person to appear in public wearing his pants below his waist and thereby exposing his skin or intimate clothing." In the town of Opelousas, Louisiana, wearing low-slung pants already garners an offender up to six months in prison.[10]

But overcriminalization is only rarely amusing—more often, it's genuinely threatening. Legislators and regulators have painted with so broad a brush that ordinary businesspeople are at risk of prosecution for everyday business activities. Justices Clarence Thomas and Sandra Day O'Connor emphasized that risk in their dissent from the Court's refusal to hear the appeal in *United States v. Hanousek* (2000). In that case, Edward Hanousek Jr., a roadmaster for a railroad company in Alaska, was sentenced to six months in prison when a backhoe operator working under him accidentally ruptured an oil pipeline while sweeping rocks off a section of track. Hanousek, who was off duty and away from the site when the accident occurred, was convicted of unlawful discharge under the Clean Water Act by reason of negligent failure to supervise. Justice Thomas, joined by Justice O'Connor, dissented from the Court's denial of review. "[T]his case," warned Thomas, "illustrates that the [Clean Water Act] . . . imposes criminal liability for persons using standard equipment to engage in a broad range of ordinary industrial and commercial activities. . . . I think we should be hesitant to expose countless numbers of construction workers and contractors to heightened criminal liability for using ordinary devices to engage in normal industrial operations."[11]

More recently, in February 2004, the Supreme Court refused to hear the appeals in *McNab v. United States* and *Blandford v. United States,* two cases in which four seafood dealers faced long federal prison terms even though they hadn't violated any law.[12] Defendants' punishment is based on the facts that (1) they improperly shipped some lobster tails in plastic bags rather than cardboard boxes, (2) some 3 percent of the lobster shipment contained lobsters with tails less than five inches long, and (3) less than 7 percent of the same shipment may have contained egg-bearing lobsters. According to the federal government, these facts constitute a "crime" under the Lacey Act, a federal statute that makes it a crime to import fish or wildlife taken "in violation of any foreign law."

There's just one problem with that theory: no foreign laws had been violated. The U.S. government claims that the shipment violated Honduran law; Honduras says otherwise. In fact, the Honduran National Human Rights Commissioner issued a legal opinion stating that the defendants had been convicted on the basis of an "error of law," and the attorney general of Honduras filed an amicus curiae brief with the federal court of appeals confirming that the defendants had not violated any Honduran law.[13] It was all to no avail. One defendant, who had been deemed a "flight risk" early on in the proceedings, has been in prison for four years as of this writing, with four left to serve. The other three will serve sentences ranging from two to eight years.

The rich and famous can fall victim to the New Criminalization as easily as can the obscure. Around the same time that the Supreme Court denied review in the lobster cases, high-profile defendant Martha Stewart's battle against federal prosecutors was coming to a close. The U.S. attorney's office for the Southern District of New York brought charges against Martha Stewart arising out of her December 27, 2001, sale of nearly 4,000 shares of ImClone stock— a sale triggered by her broker's tip that ImClone's CEO had sold his stock in the company. The prosecutors did not charge Stewart with insider trading, given that she was not an "insider" and there was no credible allegation that she'd received information directly from the CEO. Instead, they prosecuted her for making false statements to federal officials investigating the case, and for publicly proclaiming that she was innocent, an act prosecutors claimed was designed to prop up the stock price of her own company, Martha Stewart Living Omnimedia. In essence, Stewart was charged with "having misled people by denying having committed a crime with which she was not charged," as Cato Institute senior fellow Alan Reynolds put it.

On February 27, 2004, federal judge Miriam Goldman Cedarbaum threw out the securities fraud charge against Stewart because the evidence supporting "an essential element of a charged crime was 'nonexistent or so meager that no reasonable jury could find guilt beyond a reasonable doubt.'" That victory was short-lived, however. A week later, Martha Stewart was convicted on the remaining counts. In July, Stewart was sentenced to five months in federal prison and five months of home confinement.

The U.S. attorney behind the Martha Stewart prosecution, James Comey, maintained that Stewart was "prosecuted not because of who she is but because of what she did." That claim is hard to credit, given the audacious legal theory under which he pursued her.

Comey serves as a good example of how overcriminalization empowers ambitious prosecutors seeking high-publicity cases. In mid-2003, Comey even considered prosecuting fabulist Jayson Blair for the hitherto unknown crime of making stuff up in the *New York Times*. Blair, the *Times* reporter who faked stories and quotes, became the subject of scandal in early 2003 when the *Times* unearthed his deception. In May of that year, James Comey's office sought information from the *Times* as a prelude to prosecution, possibly for mail fraud—the all-purpose weapon in the prosecutorial arsenal.[14]

In the end, Comey decided not to prosecute, but it says something that he even considered making a federal case out of the Blair scandal. Apparently, those of us old-fashioned enough to think that breaches of journalistic ethics ought to be policed by journalists rather than federal prosecutors are just not in tune with federal priorities in the 21st century.

In his headline-grabbing zeal and his readiness to stretch the law, James Comey is the very model of a modern federal prosecutor. And it hasn't hurt his career. In October 2003, President Bush promoted Comey to deputy attorney general at the Justice Department, in the number two spot behind John Ashcroft.

Comey is hardly alone in his readiness to make a federal case out of almost anything. The problem is systemic, driven by legislators who are all too willing to turn every social problem into a matter for the criminal law. We are, as Harvard Law professor William Stuntz warns, coming "ever closer to a world in which the law on the books makes everyone a felon, and in which prosecutors and police both define the law on the street and decide who has violated it."[15] The book you're holding chronicles these disturbing trends.

We begin with Erik Luna's overview of the problem in his essay "Overextending the Criminal Law." Luna identifies the link between a series of seemingly disparate events, including the arrest (and handcuffing) of a 12-year-old girl caught eating fries in a Washington, D.C., Metro station and the mail fraud conviction of a college professor who awarded degrees to students who plagiarized each other's work. What links such incidents is the criminal law's shift from a shared expression of societal condemnation to an all-purpose tool of social control. It's a shift that has tragic consequences: As Luna notes, "When the criminal sanction is used for conduct that is widely viewed as harmless or undeserving of the severest condemnation, the moral force of the penal code is diminished, possibly to the point of near irrelevance among some individuals and groups."

In "The New 'Criminal' Classes: Legal Sanctions and Business Managers," James V. DeLong takes a closer look at the ongoing revolution in criminal law. With a particular emphasis on the burgeoning area of environmental crime, DeLong outlines four trends afflicting the criminal law generally. First, regulatory systems have become so complex that "no one understands them, including their enforcers." Second, *mens rea*, or evil intent, once an indispensable element of criminal offenses, is no longer required; businesspeople can be convicted, and even jailed, for behavior that barely meets the standard of negligence. Third, it is becoming increasingly difficult to avoid being subject to the dictates of the regulatory regime being created by these trends: "The new criminalization permeates every area of the economy and society," notes DeLong. Finally, a defendant prosecuted for regulatory violations will often find himself with fewer constitutional protections than a common thief or murderer. The protections of the Fourth and Fifth Amendments have been greatly undermined by the new criminalization, and, as DeLong shows, "the right to be convicted only on the basis of competent evidence is also under attack."

These developments threaten to turn America into a society that's far less dynamic and far less free. The genius of the common law system was that people who took care to act prudently and honestly might have to compensate third parties for accidental harm, but they could be reasonably sure they were safe from criminal prosecution. That regime encouraged entrepreneurial initiative and innovation. But, as DeLong explains, "The new emphasis on criminalization . . . dictates passivity, as clarification of the rules must be sought and prior approval secured. . . . The approach is disempowering, as it forces private actors to play 'Mother, May I?' with the government over each minute aspect of their businesses."

Like DeLong, Timothy Lynch focuses on environmental crimes in his contribution to the volume. In "Polluting Our Principles: Environmental Prosecutions and the Bill of Rights," Lynch paints a picture of a federal enforcement apparatus run amuck, pursuing enforcement quotas in an attempt to "get the numbers up"—regardless of justice. The environmental offenses added to the criminal code since the first Earth Day nearly 35 years ago are in some cases so vague that even environmental lawyers cannot reliably tell businesspeople whether they're at risk of prosecution. Lynch quotes one prosecutor: "When the little hairs on the back of your neck stand up, it's a felony. When it just makes you tingle, it's a misdemeanor. If it does nothing to you at all, it's a civil problem."

Of particular interest is Lynch's contention that the courts have adopted what might be called an "environmental exception" to the Bill of Rights. Key provisions of the Fourth and Fifth Amendments simply do not apply in environmental investigations and prosecutions. The Fourth Amendment's warrant requirement does not apply to closely regulated industries—even where the fruits of the search can result in criminal prosecutions. Despite the Fifth Amendment's proscription against self-incrimination, a number of environmental statutes make it a criminal offense not to report violations—subjecting the violator to prosecution for refusal to incriminate himself. And state and federal codes frequently criminalize the same underlying conduct, allowing prosecutors to cooperate to pile on duplicative charges for that conduct, in violation of the spirit, if not the letter, of the Fifth Amendment's Double Jeopardy clause.

Lynch and DeLong's focus on environmental crimes has proved prescient. That area of the law has continued to expand since their articles were written in the mid-to-late '90s. As Louisiana State University Law professor John S. Baker recently showed, environmental crimes constitute 24 of the 67 new sections and subsections added to the federal criminal code since 1997—more than 35 percent of the total growth.[16]

In the next chapter, Grace-Marie Turner documents another growth area in federal criminal law: the drive to stamp out health care fraud. In their quest to rein in abuses of Medicare and Medicaid, federal officials have adopted enforcement measures that threaten innocent health care providers. The Health Insurance Portability and Accountability Act of 1996 turns senior citizens into junior G-men, paying them to report their doctors for suspected irregularities; it also creates a substantial incentive for overenforcement, by giving the federal Fraud and Abuse Control Program a cut of the penalties it collects. Little wonder then that doctors guilty of little more than clerical errors and "incorrect coding" are swept up in the anti-fraud crusade. With tens of thousands of pages of complex federal regulations governing health care, and a Medicare bureaucracy seemingly incapable of providing reliable guidance, ordinary doctors today operate in a regulatory minefield where, as Turner puts it, "medical judgments made and services rendered become grounds for civil and criminal action."

My contribution to the volume examines the problem of rampant federalization of crime, using President George W. Bush's crime-control strategy as a jumping-off point. President Bush's key anti-crime initiative is a program called Project Safe Neighborhoods, which is designed to dramatically increase federal prosecution of gun-law violations. The violations it targets—gun possession by former felons, gun possession by drug users, and the like—are already illegal in all 50 states. Thus, there's no good reason for these crimes to be prosecuted at the federal level, given that the Constitution leaves the states with the primary responsibility for the ordinary administration of criminal justice. Project Safe Neighbor-hoods is a clever political gimmick that allows the president to counter calls for gun control by calling for enforcing the gun laws "already on the books." But the program shares the flaws that plague most federalization of crime: it violates the Tenth Amendment, clogs the federal courts, encourages a mindless zero tolerance policy, and opens the door for every special interest group in Washington to politicize criminal justice policy.

We close the book with a second piece by Erik Luna. "Misguided Guidelines" examines America's 17-year experiment with the U.S. Sentencing Guidelines, which Luna calls "a convoluted, hypertech-nical, and mechanical system that saps moral judgment from the process of punishment." "Guidelines" is a misnomer—the sentenc-ing grid enacted (and periodically revised) by the U.S. Sentencing Commission is anything but optional. The Guidelines prescribe man-datory punishment ranges for federal offenses and shift authority over sentencing from independent judges to an interested party in the proceedings—the prosecutor. Like the indiscriminate federaliza-tion of crime, the system set up by the Guidelines is opposed by the vast majority of scholars and jurists, yet it persists nonetheless out of sheer political convenience.

However, that may be about to change. On June 24, 2004, as this book was being completed, the Supreme Court issued its opinion in *Blakely v. Washington*—a case with profound implications for the future of the federal sentencing guidelines. At one stroke, the Court invalidated Washington state's determinate sentencing scheme, a system that bears great resemblance to the federal guidelines.

Blakely arose out of a kidnapping case in Washington state: defendant Robert Blakely pleaded guilty to second-degree kidnapping, a crime that under Washington law carried a maximum sentence of 53 months. But based on his finding that Blakely had acted with "deliberate cruelty," the judge increased the sentence to 90 months, pursuant to a provision of the Washington state sentencing guidelines. Because Blakely's sentence was enhanced by facts not proved to a jury of his peers, the Supreme Court held that the procedure was inconsistent with Blakely's Sixth Amendment right to trial by jury.

If that is so, then much of federal sentencing procedure is equally vulnerable, as federal judges across the country recognized in the weeks following *Blakely*. By late July 2004, three federal appeals courts had declared aspects of the federal sentencing guidelines unconstitutional, and the United States Senate had passed a resolution by unanimous consent asking the Supreme Court to resolve questions over the constitutionality of the federal sentencing guidelines.

It is not yet clear what the ultimate results of the Court's exercise in creative destruction will be. As Luna has noted, *Blakely* "does not touch any number of perversions and injustices under the sentencing guidelines." But its effect is far reaching enough to give reformers reason to hope that *Blakely* could spell the beginning of the end for federal sentencing as we know it. For that reason, it's one of the most promising developments in federal criminal law in decades.

Yet much remains to be done, as the articles collected in this volume show. There are no easy answers to the problems outlined in this book. Reining in overcriminalization and overfederalization requires judicial vigilance, legislative restraint, and a willingness to resist what Erik Luna calls the "crime-of-the-month" mentality. And to paraphrase H. L. Mencken, no one ever went broke underestimating the courage of the American political class.

But if diagnosis is the first step to recovery, then the articles in this book can help put us on that road. They document a serious and ongoing threat to the rule of law. Overcoming that threat may be challenging, but it's never been more important.

***

This book would not have been possible without the interest and encouragement of Cato founder and president Ed Crane and executive vice president David Boaz. Others who deserve thanks include Whitney Ward for her terrific attention to detail and her patience in going through multiple edits on this volume, and Parker Wallman for great work on the cover. Kelly Young provided valuable advice when this project was getting off the ground. David Boaz, who suggested the title for this collection, and Mark Moller provided valuable edits to the book's introduction, and plenty of excellent suggestions along the way. And my many conversations with Cato's Tim Lynch over the years have helped deepen my understanding of the role of the criminal law in a free society. Any errors are, of course, mine alone.

Notes

1. Lawrence M. Friedman, *A History of American Law* (New York: Touchstone Press, 1973), pp. 248, 257.

2. Task Force on Federalization of Criminal Law, American Bar Association, Criminal Justice Section, "The Federalization of Criminal Law" (1998).

3. John S. Baker Jr., "Measuring the Explosive Growth of Federal Crime Legislation," Federalist Society for Law and Public Policy Studies (2004).

4. Paul Rosenzweig, "The Over-Criminalization of Social and Economic Conduct," *Heritage Foundation Legal Memorandum*, April 17, 2003.

5. See Joseph G. Block and Nancy A. Voisin, "The Responsible Corporate Officer Doctrine—Can You Go to Jail for What You *Don't* Know?" *Environmental Law* (Fall 1992).

6. The United States has more than 2 million people behind bars, a higher percentage of its citizens than any other country. At 715 per 100,000, the United States is well ahead of its closest competitor, Russia (with 584). Connie Cass, "Report: 1 of every 75 U.S. Men in Prison," *Associated Press*, May 27, 2004; Sentencing Project "New Prison Figures Demonstrate Need for Comprehensive Reform," www.sentencingproject.org/pdfs/1044.pdf.

7. 2 U.S.C.A. §431(20)(A)(iii) (Supp. 2003).

8. Marc Kaufmann, "Worried Doctors Decry Prosecutions," *Washington Post*, December 29, 2003.

9. Dan Nephin, "Comedian Chong Sentenced on Drug Charges," *Associated Press*, September 11, 2003.

10. Bethany Thomas, "Memo to Britney: Lose the Low-Slungs," *NBC News*, May 13, 2004. www.msnbc.msn.com/id/4963512/?GT1=3319.

11. *Hanousek v. United States*, 528 U.S. 1102 (2000) (Thomas, J., dissenting).

12. Andrew Glazer, "Cliffs woman in smuggling case fails in bid to appeal to top court," *The Record* (Bergen County, NJ), February 27, 2004.

13. "*McNab v. United States:* A Lobster Tale: Invalid Foreign Laws Lead to Years in Prison," November 2003 Case Study, Overcriminalized.com (Heritage Foundation), www.overcriminalized.com/studies/2003.11_McNab.html.

14. "New York Times: Ex-reporter faces fraud inquiry," *CNN.com*, May 13, 2003.

15. William J. Stuntz, "The Pathological Politics of Criminal Law," *Michigan Law Review* 100 (December 2001): 505, 511.

16. Baker, see note 3, p. 15.

1. Overextending the Criminal Law
Erik Luna

"Nothing is certain," Ben Franklin once said, "but death and taxes." Had he lived during our time, Franklin might have added a few other certainties—and almost assuredly among them would have been the concept of "crime." By this, I am not referring to the rate of violence and unlawful deprivations of property or privacy in the United States, which ebbs and flows from year to year and decade to decade, often coinciding with dips in the economy or spikes in the number of young males in the general population. Instead, it is the troubling phenomenon of continually adding new crimes or more severe punishments to the penal code, criminalizing, recriminalizing, and overcriminalizing all forms of conduct, much of it innocuous, to the point of erasing the line between tolerable and unacceptable behavior.

Where once the criminal law might have stood as a well-understood and indisputable statement of shared norms in American society, now there is only a bloated compendium that looks very much like the dreaded federal tax code. The end results can be downright ugly: a soccer mom thrown in jail in a small Texas town for failing to wear a seatbelt; a 12-year-old girl arrested and handcuffed for eating french fries in a Metro station in Washington, D.C.; and defendants serving 25-years-to-life sentences in California prisons for, among other things, pilfering a slice of pizza.

These incidents may seem like outliers, the exceptions rather than the rule. And to be sure, every U.S. jurisdiction has on its books a set of crimes and punishments that are incontrovertible, involving acts and attendant mental states that must be proscribed to constitute a just society—murder, rape, robbery, arson, and the like. But beyond those so-called common law crimes is a seemingly endless list of behaviors that, at a minimum, do not seem well suited for the penal code and at times appear to fall within a zone of personal liberty that should be outside of the state's coercive powers. Moreover, the

1

sheer number of idiosyncratic laws and the scope of discretionary enforcement might give reason to wonder whether the exceptions have become the rule.

Some crimes barely pass the laugh test. New Mexico makes it a misdemeanor to claim that a product contains honey unless it is made of "pure honey produced by honeybees." Florida criminalizes the display of deformed animals and the peddling of untested sparklers, as well as the mutilation of the Confederate flag for "crass or commercial purposes." Pretending to be a member of the clergy is a misdemeanor in Alabama, and Kentucky bans the use of reptiles during religious services. Maine prohibits the catching of crustaceans with anything but "conventional lobster traps," and Texas declares it a felony to trip a horse or "seriously overwork" an animal. In turn, California forbids "three-card monte" and, as a general rule, cheating at card games, while it's a crime in Illinois to camp on the side of a public highway or offer a movie for rent without clearly displaying its rating. Add to those gems countless local offenses such as playing frisbee on Galveston beaches after being warned by a lifeguard; molesting monarch butterflies in Pacific Grove, California; failing to return library books in Salt Lake City; or annoying birds in the parks of Honolulu.

Less comical but certainly more pervasive and consequential are the so-called vice crimes that have exasperated generations of American libertarians. These offenses are marked by the absence of violence or coercion, with parties engaged in voluntary transactions for desired goods or services. This category would include the possession, sale, or use of illegal drugs; acts of prostitution and other commercialized sexual conduct; transactions involving pornography or allegedly obscene materials; and all kinds of gambling activities. Government has also banned behaviors that are related to vice or seen as precursors to vice, for example, the possession of drug paraphernalia such as pipes and spoons and loitering in public places with the apparent intent to sell drugs or turn tricks. Congress has even considered a bill that would make it a federal crime to throw a party where drugs might be used.

Criminalizing Business

Other growth areas for the penal code include regulatory or business-related offenses and crimes involving misrepresentation and the like. Today's administrative state has created a massive web of laws concerning trade, labor, product and workplace safety, environmental protection, securities regulation, housing, transportation, and so on, often backed by the criminal sanction. Many of the statutes may make a good deal of sense—for example, prohibiting modern iterations on the common law crime of larceny. Others seem a bit silly, such as the infamous federal crimes of removing mattress tags and the unauthorized use of "Smokey the Bear" or "Woodsy Owl." But many regulatory offenses—filing an inaccurate monitoring report under the Clean Water Act or being in a position of responsibility when an employee violates regulations of the FDA, EPA, SEC, and other acronym agencies—place otherwise honest folks in real jeopardy. As Berkeley law professor Sanford Kadish once noted, some economic crimes, such as violations of securities regulations, antitrust statutes, and unfair competition laws, more "closely resembles acceptable aggressive business behavior." In turn, mail and wire fraud statutes have been expanded to seemingly irrational ends, covering conduct that amounts to little more than breaches of fiduciary duty. In one case, a college professor was convicted of mail fraud for awarding degrees to students who plagiarized others' work.

Beyond the truly novel are offenses that merely recriminalize or overcriminalize conduct that is already prohibited. Many penal codes contain dozens of provisions covering the same basic crime—assault, theft, sex offenses, arson, and so on—each provision dealing with an allegedly unique scenario but in fact just retreading the same conduct. Politically inspired offenses fall within this category as well, with, for instance, "carjacking," which is more than well covered by proscriptions on robbery and kidnapping. Penal code machinations have also involved drastic expansions in punishment, most notably the enactment of mandatory minimum sentences for narcotics crimes and anti-recidivist statutes along the lines of "three strikes and you're out." And after factoring in various liability-expanding doctrines, such as conspiracy and solicitation, the reach and force of the criminal law and its penalties can be awe inspiring and disconcerting.

None of this is particularly new because the criminalization phenomenon has been the subject of legal commentary for decades. Legendary figures of academe such as Kadish and Stanford's Herbert

3

Packer have chronicled the American propensity to use and abuse the criminal sanction, with further refinements by distinguished contemporary scholars like Columbia's John Coffee and Harvard's William Stuntz. And yet, the phenomenon continues largely unabated: Over the past century, the number of crimes in most state penal codes has at least doubled, and there are now more than 4,000 offenses punishable as federal crimes.

Why the Urge to Criminalize?

Any number of explanations can be offered for America's drive to criminalize—its appetite for a crime-of-the-month. Part of the rationale likely stems from a slow but certain movement away from common law principles of crime and punishment and toward a larger ambit for the criminal justice system. To simplify a bit, the common law required a convergence of harmful conduct (*actus reus*) and a culpable mental state (*mens rea*). As an example, larceny involved more than just taking someone's private property—the accused must have known that the object in question belonged to another and intended to deprive him of that property. There were also fairly robust limitations on vicarious liability, whether a homeowner could be criminally culpable for the actions of his drunken visitor, for instance, or the businessman could be liable for the wrongful deeds of his employee. Today, however, criminal responsibility can be doled out without a culpable mental state through the concept of "strict liability," and corporate managers can be held liable for serious offenses without evidence of personal guilt. An honest and reasonable claim of "I didn't know" is often deemed irrelevant, despite the mind-boggling number of administrative regulations that carry criminal sanctions. This trend is only exacerbated by the slow disappearance of the line between crime and tort, with conduct that was once actionable only by civil suit now susceptible to criminal prosecution as well, oftentimes at the sole discretion of the relevant law enforcement agency. And in an age of "Enronitis," we can only expect further expansions of criminal liability for business managers and corporate executives.

Another explanation can be found in the continuing power of legal moralism and its transformation in popular discourse. Almost all vice crimes stem from religious-based conceptions of good and evil. Drugs, alcohol, gambling, prostitution, adultery, fornication,

4

sodomy, pornography, and other obscenities are banned by the state on the basis of notions of human wickedness and righteousness and, ultimately, the desire to reform society in accord with puritanical or Victorian standards. Some of these crimes have fallen by the wayside with, for example, the end of Prohibition in 1933 and, more recently, a variety of statutory or constitutional changes on issues of sex and sexuality. But drug crimes continue to be added or augmented in modern penal codes, and some jurisdictions have created new sex- and gambling-related offenses, although not expressly as a result of religious moralizing. Instead, proponents argue that such behaviors cause "harm" not only to the direct participants but to the greater community as well. To see an alleged prostitute or drug dealer on the streets produces a type of social harm sufficient to justify the full force of the criminal justice system, or so it is claimed.

Probably the most powerful explanation for the criminalization phenomenon is the one-way ratchet of law-and-order politics. To put it simply, lawmakers have every reason to add new crimes and punishments, which make great campaign fodder, but no countervailing political interest in cutting the penal code. The benefits of overcriminalization are concentrated on the political class, providing nice sound bites and résumé filler at reelection time, while the costs are either diffuse (but very real, as will be discussed below) or borne by discrete and insular minorities without sway in the political process, such as members of lower socioeconomic classes or those accused of crime. Experience has shown that being tough on crime wins elections, and a sure-fire way to look tough is to add a superfluous carjacking statute or boost the penalty for drug dealers, irrespective of the statute's normative justification or ultimate effect on society. And once on the books, criminal laws are virtually impossible to rescind (consider, for instance, the continued existence of anti-dueling statutes).

Law enforcement officials also contribute to criminalization binges. As Professor Stuntz has noted, the more crimes on the books, the more conduct prohibited (and prohibited in more ways), and the more punishment for a given crime, the more authority police and prosecutors can exert in the criminal justice system. Imagine that law enforcement is pursuing a crime that is composed of three elements: X, Y, and Z. If Z happens to be difficult to observe on the streets or prove in court, then law enforcement may well want a

5

new crime composed of only two elements, X and Y. In similar fashion, if crime A carries only a fine or a short jail term, criminal defendants may lack an incentive to enter into plea bargaining with officials. But if a new law adds five years of prison time for crime A, creates a new crime B that covers roughly the same conduct yet carries a 15-year sentence, or establishes a life-imprisonment scheme for repeat offenders, law enforcement now has a blunt instrument that will often leave the accused little choice but to negotiate a guilty plea.

The Costs of Overcriminalization

The costs and consequences of overcriminalization are many and, in many cases, all too obvious—but let me briefly mention a few. To begin with, a bloated penal code and overly broad criminal liability are unhealthy for an adversarial system of criminal justice in which law enforcers are not neutral and detached but instead interested parties actively seeking arrests and convictions. Overcriminalization leads to enormous police discretion to stop pedestrians or motorists by using legal pretexts that serve as cover for discriminatory enforcement based on class, race, or ethnicity. As observed by racial profiling scholar David Harris, no driver could cover more than three blocks without violating some traffic law, thereby providing a pretense for a prolonged detention and extensive search. For prosecutors, overcriminalization results in a total imbalance of arms, with severe punishment, often in the form of mandatory minimums or habitual offender statutes, used as leverage in extracting information or guilty pleas. Prosecutorial domination via overcriminalization is bad enough when the underlying offense and attached penalties are dubious to begin with (drug crimes being the paradigmatic case for libertarians like myself). But the sledgehammer of draconian punishment is most disturbing when it is used to coax pleas out of individuals with valid claims of mitigation or even innocence, an unsettling situation that has proven to be all too common.

Overcriminalization also has the potential to squander or misallocate scarce resources, particularly when the underlying offense—a vice crime, for example—causes little direct harm. "One can imagine side effects of the effort to enforce morality by penal law," Professor Louis Schwartz of the University of Pennsylvania wondered some 40 years ago. "Are police forces, prosecution resources, and court time being wastefully diverted from the central insecurities of our metropolitan life—robbery, burglary, rape, assault, and governmental corruption?'' The answer is the same today as it was then: Resources spent chasing the otherwise innocuous prostitute and panderer, for instance, could be spent instead in pursuit of the real sex criminals—the rapist and the child molester. And, of course, the billions of dollars wasted on the so-called war on drugs would be better spent on a different, much graver battle: the ''war on terror'' and the pursuit of those who would fly commercial airliners into American skyscrapers; set off bombs in public venues and government buildings; and release biochemical weapons through mail, commerce, or public works.

Most of all, overcriminalization weakens the moral force of the criminal law. By ''moral,'' I am not referring to big-M *Morality*, as in the occasionally obnoxious religiosity of the ''Moral Majority,'' but instead the shared norms of American society as to what should or should not be subject to the single most powerful action any government can take: the deprivation of human liberty or even life itself. That is, after all, what a penal code should be about—a communal decision that certain behaviors, pursuant to certain mental states, are so violent or harmful to their direct victims and society at large as to justify the social reprobation and deprivation of liberty that accompany the adjudication of guilt. When the criminal sanction is used for conduct that is widely viewed as harmless or undeserving of the severest condemnation, the moral force of the penal code is diminished, possibly to the point of near irrelevance among some individuals and groups. It fails to distinguish between the acceptable and the intolerable, between the lawful and the illicit. And it no longer deters *ex ante*, before crime, but only catalogs punishment *ex post*, at trial and at sentencing when the damage has already been done. Unwarranted bans or penalties can fulfill none of the valid goals of the criminal sanction, namely, preventing future harmful conduct and justly punishing individuals for past wrongdoing.

Before another offense or punishment is added to the penal code, we should start asking ourselves, *Is this really necessary or just another crime-of-the-month?*

Originally published in Cato Policy Report, Vol. XXV, No. 6, November/ December 2003.

2. The New "Criminal" Classes: Legal Sanctions and Business Managers

James V. DeLong

Distrust all in whom the impulse to punish is powerful.
—Friedrich Nietzsche[1]

The Impulse to Punish

Concern with crime and faith in punishment are usually associated with political conservatives, who are likely to advocate longer sentences, oppose restrictions on the use of evidence, favor limits on habeas corpus, and complain about soft judges. In contrast, self-classified liberals are typically skeptical about punitive measures and talk of root causes and the need for social justice.

Half of this stereotype is growing obsolete. The political Left may retain its doubts about punishment in the context of street crimes, but in other areas it is spearheading a spectacular expansion in the scope and intensity of the nation's apparatus for punishment. Multiple provisions for penalties are routine parts of every new regulatory proposal. The new regime arising from this impulse to punish, which has given birth to criminal penalties in the areas of environmental protection, financial practices, government contracting, employment relations, civil rights, medical practice—indeed every area of government interaction with society and the economy—is what I call the "New Criminalization." A decade ago, an estimated 300,000 federal regulations could be enforced through criminal penalties.[2] Who knows what the number is now.

In the environmental area alone, no federal statute called for felony sanctions until the 1980s. All statutes passed since then contain serious criminal penalties, and by early 1995 the Department of Justice had indicted 443 corporations and 1,068 individuals, convicted 334 organizations and 740 individuals, recovered $297 million in criminal penalties, and obtained sentences of imprisonment totaling 561 years.[3] States do even more. The great bulk of environmental

9

enforcement is at the state level, and, according to one analysis, "state environmental criminal prosecutions are several orders of magnitude more numerous than their federal counterparts."[4]

Appreciating the true strength of this movement requires attention to more than the expansion in criminal laws and sanctions, however. Punitive "civil" enforcement provisions, such as forfeiture of property, monetary penalties, treble damages, punitive damages, debarment from doing business with the government, and exaggerated estimates of compensatory damages have grown apace. In the environmental area alone, the EPA has collected more than $3 billion in such fines.[5] More than 100 different forfeiture-of-property provisions are in effect. The promotion of private actions through bounties is also a new and expanding frontier. The False Claims Act, originally passed during the Civil War, gives whistleblowers a share of any money recovered from a government contractor, and the law was expanded in 1986 to make recoveries easier. Its application also extends far beyond the defense contracting business into health care and even environmental law. If these specific regulatory regimes are not enough, lawyers keep pushing to expand the federal Racketeer Influenced and Corrupt Organizations Statute (RICO), with its treble damages and forfeiture provisions, into new crannies of activity.

Yet another way in which the system has become more punitive is through the increased legal costs of defending an action. Most of the regulatory structures are incredibly complex, which makes legal defense extraordinarily expensive. A minimum of $100,000 is necessary to mount any kind of case, and the costs escalate from there.[6] The assets of any normal family are quickly exhausted. Most people find financial ruin more painful than a few weeks of community service or even jail, and a rational defendant often will choose to plead guilty rather than defend and go bankrupt.

From a commonsense point of view, all these not-quite-criminal sanctions are an integral part of the punitive system. They share the most basic characteristic of criminal sanctions: they are intended to cause pain, not simply to compensate for damage. A counterargument can be made that some systems of civil penalties, such as the one administered by the Environmental Protection Agency, are designed only to remove the profit from an environmental violation. However, few practitioners believe this. The deck is stacked to make the price high, and the basic goal is really deterrence.[7]

The only serious opposition to this trend, indeed, almost the only notice of it outside of a few references in law reviews, comes from a coalition of political libertarians and civil liberties advocates. The business classes, normally regarded as conservative, demonstrate a quiescence that is remarkable considering their role as the primary targets of this movement. It seems as if the Left and the Right have entered into an agreement whereby each side gets to criminalize conduct it abhors so long as it lets the other do the same. Restrictions on parole for muggers are balanced by jail sentences for violators of obscure regulations on wetlands or endangered species. Increases in the number of federal offenses subject to capital punishment are matched by forfeiture of the assets of individuals accused of soliciting sex or of doctors who misread complicated health care rules. More money for prison construction is approved on the condition that a number of the cells be reserved for the newly criminalized managerial and professional and entrepreneurial classes.

The breadth and intensity of this wholesale adoption of punitive measures are impressive. Reading the daily newspaper has become like subscribing to a service called the "Professional, Managerial, and Entrepreneurial Classes Crime Report." When one probes beneath the surface of these examples, disturbing trends appear. It is always possible to find examples of genuinely reprehensible conduct, of course. The growth in the size and complexity of our society provides many new opportunities for chicanery, and human ingenuity is rising to the challenge. But we have gone far beyond punishing instances of one person harming another physically or taking unfair advantage of others through trickery or fraud. We have reached the point where government regulators punish matters that are, at root, contract disputes, or uncertainties over legal or moral requirements, or confusion over tradeoffs among competing values (such as land preservation versus new homes), or simply the normal ruck of error inherent in human affairs. Darker forces are also at work, as special interests no longer limit themselves to raiding the treasury for subsidies or special treatment in the tax code; they capture regulatory agencies and processes, and use the punitive enforcement powers of the government as the mechanism to transfer benefits to themselves or to enforce pet ideas of virtue.

Here are some gleanings of recent clippings, plucked out of a staggering list of possibilities:

- In FY95, the EPA made 256 criminal referrals and 214 civil referrals to the Department of Justice and imposed 1,105 administrative penalty orders. It collected $94 million in fines and penalties and imposed injunctive relief and other environmental requirements worth $1.1 billion. In FY96, it made 262 criminal referrals, collected $173 million in fines and penalties, and persuaded polluters to spend $1.49 billion to correct violations and prevent future problems.[8]
- Environmental enforcement is not directed solely at large corporations and their officers. Individuals are targeted in their roles as landowners, waste generators, or small business owners or operators. The definition of a wetland is so expansive that people have been convicted of "filling in wetlands" for putting clean dirt on dry land.[9] A developer in Charles County, Maryland, continued a development that had been under construction since 1968 with the full approval of all state and local authorities. The development is on the highest elevation in the county in the middle of an urban area, and the Army Corps of Engineers approved it in 1976. None of this mattered because the developer was sentenced to 21 months in jail for "filling in a wetland."[10] And in the Duell case in New York, a husband and wife were each sentenced to six months in jail and a joint fine of $340,000 for a leaky septic tank that may not have actually polluted any waters. They also lost their property under the financial pressure.[11]
- The health care company SmithKline Beecham paid $325 million to settle allegations that it had cheated the government on Medicare charges. The company says that the matter stems from ambiguities in the language of regulations and guidelines, and that any errors were inadvertent. However, it adds, the costs and risks of fighting it out were too great, and prudence dictated a settlement.[12]
- Medicare pays for hospice care only for patients with less than six months to live. The government is distressed because patients in some hospices are living longer than this. Although at least 90 percent die within six months, a few last longer. The government's position is that this must be fraud—and the government is out to get money back from these cheating institutions that keep their patients alive too long.[13]

- Judge Ralph Winter of the Second Circuit notes that corporate officers are now subject to criminal penalties for failing to give a sufficiently accurate account to the company of their activities. But there are no established standards. The crime is simply invented by the particular jury. It is not a defense that the officer intended no wrong, or that the company suffered no loss, or that nobody relied on the failure to disclose, or that the nondisclosure involved only trivia.[14]

- A former university president was a director of an S&L. In 1992, he became a defendant in a $32 million suit. The law firm prosecuting the case for the government sent him a letter noting that if he wanted to settle, "the RTC is likely to approve a settlement significantly less than the collective cost of hiring counsel to present a defense on your behalf. . . . All in all, it is a very complex and highly stressful process." He fought for four years, then settled for $20,000.[15] One former S&L director or officer not in jail and not paying anything is Henry Hyde, Chairman of the Committee on the Judiciary of the U.S. House of Representatives. He refused to contribute to a settlement on the grounds that he did nothing wrong.[16] He is believable because, aside from his personal credibility, it is safe to assume the prosecutors left no stone unturned in looking for sin. But how many of the other 6,405 defendants could have made a similar claim but lacked either the resources to mount a defense or the power and visibility to ensure that any case against them would receive close scrutiny?

- The Philadelphia-based law firm Morgan, Lewis & Bockius has been sued for $100 million by the State of Pennsylvania for "civil racketeering" under RICO. The firm has plenty of company. As of 1992, 2,000 civil RICO suits were pending against lawyers and accountants alone, and "ordinary commercial disputes pled as RICO claims are now commonplace."[17]

- Private-sector members are not the only ones at risk, because becoming a government employee is growing perilous. The ill-defined and suspiciously makeweight crimes of lying to Congress or to a federal investigator have become familiar. Federal officials are subject to penalties for violation of many ethical rules, including failure to disclose minutiae of personal financial affairs.

Analyzing the Trend

The application of punitive sanctions to a large-scale industrial society and welfare state in which the government intrudes into every nook and cranny is creating serious problems. These can be grouped into four major categories, which will be summarized, then taken up in more detail.

- *Increased Complexity.* Regulatory systems have become incredibly complex, to the point where no one understands them, including their enforcers. Further, a good moral sense is no guide; many of the requirements are *malum prohibitum* (wrong because it is prohibited), not *malum in se* (wrong in and of itself).
- *Diminished Role of Intent.* The government has persuaded the courts to dilute the great bulwark of *mens rea*, or evil intent, as an element of criminal offenses, and to ignore it completely for "civil" penalties, even those that have a fiercely punitive impact. People are now absolutely liable for complex and often incomprehensible requirements.
- *Greater Intrusiveness.* Few members of the professional, managerial, or entrepreneurial classes can avoid the requirements of the new regulatory regime. The New Criminalization permeates every area of the economy and society. The one group not much impacted so far is journalists, which may explain why the phenomenon has received so little attention.
- *Diminished Constitutional Protections.* Unlike a standard criminal, such as a murderer or robber, someone involved in one of the new-style offenses often cannot decline to incriminate himself, has serious difficulty protecting against arbitrary searches and seizures, and can make only limited use of the attorney-client privilege. Standards for what constitutes credible evidence also are being lowered.

Increased Complexity

Again, this section draws primarily on environmental law for its examples. However, there is no reason to think that the trends working in the environmental area differ from those in other fields, and occasional examples are invoked as a reminder of that fact.

There are at least 25 major environmental statutes in effect. All provide for criminal penalties (jail and fines) as well as for civil monetary penalties. Some penalty sections are keyed to specific statutory duties, but for the most part they are general catchall provisions that apply to any violation of the law or its implementing regulations. Extra penalties apply to particularly egregious offenses.

This scattergun approach subjects even venial sins to criminal sanctions. Under the Clean Air Act, any violation of any regulation issued by a state or the federal government is a crime. Recordkeeping is governed by regulations, so filling out a form incorrectly is an offense, as is any other failure. This may seem like a minor point; surely the government would not act unjustly. But the government does pursue technical violations, especially if it is convinced the target is guilty of more serious wrongs but lacks the evidence to prove the graver offenses. In addition, bureaucracies are always under pressure to justify their budgets by producing numbers demonstrating accomplishment. Anyone who thinks bureaucrats do not succumb to the temptation to pick up easy numbers by prosecuting or charging trivial but easily provable offenses is guilty of excessive naivete.

Nor are prosecutors totally free agents on these matters. Professor Richard Lazarus—no foe of strong environmental enforcement—has written in detail about the government decision not to prosecute in connection with pollution at the weapons factory at Rocky Flats in Colorado.[18] The reward for prosecutors who acted with a sophisticated regard for the complexities and moral nuances of the situation, in accord with what one would think are highly desirable standards of ethical behavior, was excoriation by Congress and the press. The lesson will not be lost. It is inevitable that open-ended prosecutorial discretion will eventually become a shuttlecock of sound-bite politics.

The structure of the environmental protection statutes multiplies the problems caused by the offhand breadth of the penalty sections. The laws are an amalgam of congressional micromanagement specifying minute detail on some topics combined with limitless delegation to the EPA on others. They apply across the board to a multitude of industries and organizations, and the requirements usually mesh poorly with the operational needs of any particular industry. Every term and concept is subject to endless debate and interpretation.

A good example is the Resource Conservation and Recovery Act (RCRA), which governs hazardous waste. The statute is detailed, complex, and obscure. It applies to hundreds of thousands of wildly different business entities, and delegates great power to the EPA. The law's basic definitions of hazardous waste are confusing, and the implementing regulations are circular gibberish. Other regulations are almost as opaque. An important EPA purpose under RCRA is actually to decrease industrial efficiency. The EPA wants to raise the costs of generating hazardous waste, thus discouraging activities involving such waste, regardless of any risks presented to humans or the environment. This Luddite philosophy makes the agency's reasoning particularly convoluted and difficult to follow.

An illustration of RCRA-think, by no means an unusual one, is a document that has become famous as "the solvent letter."[19] Spent solvent is one category of hazardous waste. If you clean a piece of machinery by putting solvent on the machine, wiping it down with a rag, and then tossing the rag in the trash, you are committing a number of criminal offenses. The solvent becomes "spent" when it eats the grease, so wiping it up with the rag transfers this hazardous waste to the rag. By tossing it out you dispose of hazardous waste without a permit. If, however, you pour the solvent on the rag first and then wipe the machine, you might still be a citizen in good standing. The solvent is not spent when it is poured on the rag, so wiping the machine with the rag does not entail transferring hazardous waste to the rag. If you then toss the rag in the trash, you are disposing of hazardous waste only if the discarded material would flunk specific EPA tests for "the characteristic of toxicity." Whether the test should be applied only to the solvent contained in the rag or to the combination of grease, rag, and solvent is a weighty and unsettled point. It has remained unsettled for more than 20 years.

The solvent letter is an informal memorandum, not a rule or even a guidance document. In RCRA and in every other area, the EPA and the states work through a mishmash of policy pronouncements embodied in the fine print of *Federal Register* notices, guidance documents, judicial opinions and their exegeses, thousands of letters of agency interpretations, verbal advice given over the hot line by employees of EPA contractors, and positions taken in civil and criminal enforcement actions. Arguably, all these constitute interpretations of the statute and its regulations, so one risks hefty penalties and jail if one violates any of them, no matter how casually created or contradictory of other interpretations.

The EPA also routinely uses the complexity and ambiguity of the statutory language to expand its authority as far as possible. RCRA is an example of this phenomenon, as the EPA uses a law directed at disposal of hazardous waste as a mandate to extend its authority deep into the workings of industrial processes. Consider, too, the Clean Water Act (CWA), a textbook case of the possibilities open to creative interpreters of legal language. The statute is directed at controlling the "discharge of pollutants into the navigable waters [of the United States]." You may think you know what this means— "do not dump your industrial waste into the nearest river." However, it has gone way beyond that. In the government's view, "navigable waters" include any waters that connect to navigable waters, a proposition upheld by the Supreme Court. "Waters of the United States" also include waters that *do not* connect with navigable waters. For a time, even the EPA hesitated at asserting this, but in 1985 General Counsel Frank Blake hit on the answer. He signed an opinion that the CWA covered isolated waters that could be used by migrating birds or endangered species.[20] The validity of using peripatetic birds as a fount of agency power in a statute based on navigable waters has been a subject of solemn judicial consideration ever since, and remains unresolved.

The jurisdiction of the CWA can be stretched still further. Groundwater connects with surface water, though it may take a few thousand years, so a discharge that affects groundwater also might be within the ambit of the Clean Water Act. If you stand on your patio and pour the dregs of your drink on the ground, in the view of the U.S. government, you may have committed a criminal act.

So far, the government is not busting patio parties. But it has used these authorities aggressively to convert the Clean Water Act into a nationwide program of wetlands protection, and it does indeed prosecute. As Roger Marzulla, a leading expert on property rights, has noted, "For years now, the Corps of Engineers and the EPA have operated the wetlands program as though a statute existed which makes it a felony to disturb wetlands. Congress may well believe that such a program should exist; if so, it must pass that statute in accordance with Constitutional procedures. . . . Unelected bureaucracies . . . cannot be allowed to make up the rules as they go along." Nonetheless, between January 1990 and May 1992 alone, the Justice Department prosecuted 47 corporations and individuals for criminal wetlands violations.[21] The tempo has not eased since then. Because of the expansive scope given the Clean Water Act, the term "wetlands" has expanded to include property that no one in his right mind would regard as included. Even with the best will in the world, no one can tell what is within the definition. As I wrote in 1997:

> [D]efining a legally controlled wetland is a judgment call. In the words of an [Army Corps of Engineers] official, "for regulatory purposes, a wetland is whatever we decide it is." It is also a moving target. Between 1986 and 1994 the basic definition of wetlands used by the government changed at least six times. To really explore this question would require an explanation of the Corps of Engineers Manual of 1987, the 1989 revision, the 1991 compromise, the Congressional action blocking the use of the 1989 revision and mandating a return to the 1987 version, the National Research Council Report of 1995, and several Memoranda of Agreement between the Corps and EPA. You might even want to start with the Swamp Act of 1850 and work your way forward through the 1956 Fish and Wildlife Service definition, the 1979 Cowardin Report, and other primary sources. For a short cut, call the Environmental Law Institute (ELI) in Washington, D.C., and buy its *Wetlands Deskbook*, published in 1993. This lays out the field, 661 pages of fine print of explanation, analysis, statutes, regulations, guidance letters, interagency agreements, and other documents. Then get ELI's 1996 articles updating the explanations in the 1993 work. (Things change fast.) Add a few *Federal Register* notices published in the last three years, the 1995 National Research Council report on wetlands, some Congressional hearings, and you will be ready to go.[22]

Wherever one turns in environmental law, one finds comparable complexity, technicality, indeterminacy, obscurity, and intragovernmental fragmentation and conflict.[23]

Diminished Role of Intent

Historically, intent has been a crucial part of the criminal law. Punishment is warranted only if the defendant knew the nature of his action and meant to perform it. Questions of proof sometimes have been difficult, and sometimes the necessary intent must be presumed from the nature of the act. On the one hand, it is difficult to defend on the grounds that you did not know that bullets shot from a gun are deadly. On the other hand, if a defendant were an aboriginal who had no idea what a gun was, then pointing it at someone and pulling the trigger would not demonstrate any intent to harm.

Before the current boom in criminalization, some acts were made criminal on a strict liability basis; intent was not an element of the offense. For the most part, however, the number of such offenses was limited, applying only to minor offenses bearing light penalties. These can be readily explained as cases in which avoiding an occasional minor injustice was not worth the transaction costs of requiring proof of intent. Since neither serious moral condemnation nor significant financial costs were involved, the tradeoff was viewed as acceptable.

The criminal environmental statutes almost all require that the offense be "knowing," but the meaning of that term is diluted. In *United States v. International Minerals & Chemical Co.*,[24] the Supreme Court in 1971 held that environmental crimes are "public welfare" offenses. This means that a defendant's knowledge that he is dealing with a substance known to be dangerous and thus likely to be regulated is sufficient to support a conviction even if he is unaware that he is violating the law. This formulation has caused immense problems because the government has tried to push the "you should have known it was regulated" argument to the utmost limits of its logic. In the modern world, everything is regulated, which would remove the intent requirement from the law entirely.

In some contexts, the Court has resisted this effort to dilute the *mens rea* requirement, holding that an activity that can be undertaken for innocent reasons cannot be criminalized without a showing of specific intent to violate the law. In *Staples*, a 1994 firearms case, Justice Ginsberg posed the dilemma in the following terms:

> The question before us is not *whether* knowledge of possession is required, but what level of knowledge suffices: (1) knowledge simply of possession of the object; (2) knowledge, in addition, that the object is a dangerous weapon; (3) knowledge, beyond dangerousness, of the characteristics that render the object subject to regulation, for example, awareness that the weapon is a machine gun.[25]

In *Staples*, the Court held that the defendant was culpable only if he knew that the firearm was a machine gun.[26] Three other 1994

19

Supreme Court cases addressed the issue in other contexts, with roughly similar results.[27]

The Supreme Court has not taken up the issue of intent in the context of an environmental law since *International Minerals*. Thus the basic public welfare rationale still holds, and the issue of intent raises four intertwined sets of issues:

1. *Mistake of fact*: What if the defendant thinks he knows what he is discharging, and thinks it is water?
2. *Mistake of law*: What if the defendant knows he is discharging a pollutant, but thinks the discharge is legal?
3. *Recklessness*: What if the defendant neither knows nor cares what he is discharging?
4. *Fair notice*: What if the defendant tried to do the right thing, inquired into the law and/or the facts, and was misled? What if he was misled by bad advice from regulatory authorities or by ambiguities in the regulations? Is there a requirement of "fair notice," possibly even a constitutional requirement?

The position of the U.S. government is that all of these things should be regarded as irrelevant. In *International Minerals*, the Court indicated that a defendant's genuine belief that he was discharging water might be a defense. Nonetheless, in *United States v. Ahmad*,[28] the government took the position that Ahmad could not defend on the grounds that he thought he was discharging water. In *United States v. Weitzenhoff*,[29] the government argued that the defendants should not be excused even if they honestly thought their discharges were allowed by the permit. In a Texas case, a company complied with a state interpretation issued in 1984. In 1994, the EPA said it disagreed with the state and wanted penalties of up to $25,000 per day, going back 10 years.[30]

The courts are in disarray over these challenges. In *Ahmad*, the Fifth Circuit allowed the mistake-of-fact defense. In *Weitzenhoff*, the Ninth Circuit upheld the government. Some defendants have argued for a formal "right to fair notice" doctrine, which would say, more or less, that ignorance of the law is indeed an excuse if a reasonable person cannot figure out the rules after making reasonable efforts. Due process is usually invoked to support the "fair notice" concept. A few successes are recorded, but on the whole this line of argument has not been successful. The courts keep *saying* that a defendant is entitled to reasonable notice, but in practice people are presumed to understand masses of incredibly confused rules. In at least one case, the defendant's confusion was treated as a reason to impose the penalty rather than mitigate it. The court feared that defendants would "game" the system by not applying for permits just because they could not tell whether they were supposed to do so.[31]

One court sympathetic to the fair notice argument is the D.C. Circuit. In *Rollins Environmental Services v. EPA*,[32] it held that civil penalties should not be imposed under conditions of regulatory confusion. In *General Electric v. EPA*,[33] the point was reiterated. The opinion upheld EPA's interpretation of a murky rule, but reversed EPA's attempt to impose a civil penalty on the grounds that fair notice was lacking.[34] However, the D.C. Circuit seems unique. Most courts actually overread the Supreme Court's opinion in *International Minerals*, and assume that the case foreclosed arguments for limiting the public welfare doctrine that were, in fact, left open.[35]

Nor have courts integrated into environmental enforcement the "innocent activity" problem recognized in *Staples*. Building a house on land that appears bone dry to the naked eye can be an intentional, and criminal, filling-in of wetland, despite the fact that building homes seems like an innocent activity. As a dissenting judge in *Weitzenhoff* said:

> Hot water, rock, and sand are classified as "pollutants" by the Clean Water Act. . . . Discharging silt from a stream back into the same stream may amount to discharge of a pollutant. For that matter, so may skipping a stone into a lake. So may a cafeteria worker's pouring hot, stale coffee down the drain. Making these acts a misdemeanor is one thing, but a felony is quite another . . . .[36]

The dilution of the intent requirement, combined with the uncertainty of the regulatory confusion defense, greatly enhances the government's punitive power. Environmental law has six levels of punishment: two levels of administrative penalties, judicially imposed civil penalties, misdemeanor offenses, felony indictments, and aggravated felony charges for "knowing endangerment." If intent is immaterial to the definition of the offense, then the government's burden of proof is basically the same for each of the first five levels. Deciding which of these levels to invoke is up to the prosecutor, who can choose whether a given action should result in a felony indictment or in a modest penalty assessment. The government's burden is probably higher for an offense of "knowing endangerment," but even this is not absolutely certain.[37]

Internal EPA guidelines list the factors relevant to a decision about which level of prosecution to invoke. These guidelines list the considerations one would expect to find: degree of knowledge, extent of the contamination or the seriousness of any hazard, compliance history, and the need to abate ongoing pollution.[38] However, such standards remain vague and subject to manipulation.

Moreover, the listed standards do not include several factors that experienced defense lawyers regard as relevant in the hardball world of criminal law. One factor not listed in the guidance documents is that an environmental violator who questions the agency's good faith, competence, or basic authority is much more likely to be indicted. For example, Ocie Mills in Florida was essentially jailed for insolence. He bought his lot from a relative, who had been told by the federal Army Corps of Engineers that it was a wetland. It did not look like a wetland to Mills, so he had Florida's Department of Environmental Services (DES) do a wetlands survey. The state team erected flags dividing upland from wetland, and Mills began putting sand on the upland side. The Corps sent him a letter telling him to stop. The letter included the phone number of the Florida DES to call with any questions. Mills called the DES, which said there was no problem. Mills wrote the Corps about the DES response, waited a year and heard nothing, assumed the problem resolved, and began putting more sand on the upland side of the flags. The Corps again told him to stop and again told him to call the Florida DES with any questions. Mills wrote to the Corps again, and, in the words of his lawyer, he "suggested . . . that it get its act together and get a more competent authority such as a court to straighten the matter out." He waited six months, heard nothing, put more sand on his lot, and was prosecuted and sent to jail for 21 months.[39]

Joseph Wilson, the Maryland developer sentenced to 21 months in prison in 1996, appears to be in the same category. He began his development in the 1970s. His plans were reviewed without objection by four federal agencies, including the U.S. Army Corps of Engineers. In 1990, the Corps informed Wilson that he had violated the Clean Water Act by adding fill dirt to a five-acre site that lies in the middle of a local business district, surrounded by highways and railroad tracks. Wilson removed the dirt, then sued the government, claiming that his property had effectively been taken. Only then did the government start a criminal investigation, and in 1995 it indicted Wilson for actions between 1988 and 1993 in filling in the parcel that was the subject of the original dispute and three others. All four pieces of land are urban, lie at the highest point in the county, and are more than 6 miles from the Potomac River and 10 miles from the Chesapeake Bay.[40]

If internal guidelines neglect to specify "insufficient servility" as a factor for prosecutors to consider, neither do they include "willingness to pay ransom." However, the government is reaping lots of money for something called Supplemental Environmental Projects (SEPs). SEPs are projects to improve the environment, ranging from reducing the release of pollutants to providing environmental amenities. As the EPA's Enforcement Report puts it,

> EPA uses SEPs to gain significant environmental benefits in conjunction with the settlement of enforcement cases. Nominally, SEPs are projects voluntarily undertaken by members of the regulated community in conjunction with case settlements. . . . In exchange . . . the facility is granted penalty relief. . . . Historically applied predominantly in reporting violation cases, SEPs are maturing into a more versatile tool. . . .[41]

The completeness of the prosecutorial discretion that results from the dilution of intent, combined with the complexity of the offenses, the vagueness of the stated guidelines, and the influence of important unstated factors, gives enforcement an eerie uncertainty. Legal seminars are given by current government enforcers teamed with lawyers and consultants in private practice, most of whom were enforcers until they left the government a year or so ago. These experts describe the vast powers of the agency and explain that the laws are so extensive and complicated that no business can be in compliance all the time. It is literally impossible. Corporate lawyers agree. In a recent survey, more than two-thirds of corporate attorneys conceded that their companies had violated some environmental statute during the preceding year, due largely to uncertainty and complexity.[42]

The impossibility of total compliance is not a serious problem, the seminar speakers add, because the government is reasonable and would never act unjustly, but one really does need a savvy guide through the maze. They are right about the need for a savvy guide, but corporate managers and individual entrepreneurs become unhappy when the government says, in effect, "We have created a system too complicated to understand and impossible to comply with, and all aspects of its administration—including whether to put you in jail—are totally at the discretion of the government, but do not worry because we are reasonable." Thomas Adams, a former enforcement chief at the EPA says, "Increasingly, it is clear that the government is *not* always reasonable. The system really has gone amok, and matters that used to be treated as civil, and that should be dealt with as disagreements or misunderstandings, are now crimes."[43]

Concern over this formless, standardless, and perplexing structure is deepened by additional factors. Corporations can be found guilty of criminal activities even when the acts performed were explicitly against company policy. The penalties also apply to individuals, not just organizations. The EPA emphasizes individual liability because organizations cannot go to jail and may treat monetary payments as a cost of doing business; individuals are more sensitive.

The EPA is also a strong supporter of vicarious liability, which means that it tries to penalize hierarchical superiors regardless of their knowledge or participation in any violation. Its goal is to avert management by wink or by deliberate ignorance, and to ensure that superiors conscious of their own jeopardy spare no expense complying with the regulatory requirements. Most cases against corporate officers rest on the theory that the person directed the violation, knew of it and did nothing, or remained deliberately ignorant. The government has tried to push its theories still further and to hold any "responsible corporate officer" criminally responsible. So far, the courts have resisted the effort to make individual corporate officials absolutely criminally liable on the basis of *respondeat superior*. However, courts have allowed liability to be imposed based on very little actual knowledge. For example, a corporate treasurer's opposition to a budget request for funds to remedy an alleged environmental violation may be enough to impose criminal responsibility upon her.[44]

This enforcement philosophy makes individual employees frequent targets. From the individual's point of view, given the hundreds of thousands of dollars required to defend a case of any

24

complexity, the initial targeting by government regulators is as cata-strophic as the final outcome. The necessary resources are well beyond the means of most individuals. These financial problems are exacerbated for ordinary people by an explicit government policy that treats companies that support and aid accused employees more harshly.[45]

Greater Intrusiveness

Most people, faced with a punitive structure that is complex, unpredictable, and arbitrary, react rationally by avoiding involve-ment. For conventional crimes, this works. Most people do not come close to murder, robbery, arson, or similar wrongs in their daily lives. There are always gray areas where the legal and illegal merge, and tricky distinctions are occasionally necessary, but for the most part, avoiding these offenses is not something to which respectable people must devote a great deal of thought.

With regulatory crimes, this strategy no longer works. The new burdens are omnipresent, pushing so deeply into the daily life of the managerial, professional, and entrepreneurial classes that it has become impossible to avoid skirting, and almost certainly falling over, the edge of criminality. The new structure of criminal sanctions controls, in detail, the activities that people must and are entitled to engage in, such as earning a living.

Again, the pervasive nature of the environmental laws is a good illustration. Every manager or entrepreneur in any industrial, agricultural, or extractive industry is at risk. Every home builder is in jeopardy from the wetlands and endangered species laws, and nothing in the objective situation will automatically alert him to the degree of danger. If there is no definitive way to tell whether one's property is a wetland, and knowledge and intent are irrelevant, then even the act of building or buying a home becomes perilous. Virtually everyone is at risk of prosecution.

Again, the environmental area is not unique. Any participant in the health care or defense industries is vulnerable to misreading a contract and having the dispute turn into a criminal investigation. The head of the federal Office of Thrift Supervision noted in 1992 that, as a result of all the prosecutions of S&L directors, financial institutions were having trouble attracting qualified directors. He also noted that the fear of personal liability was causing bankers to turn down creditworthy loans to creditworthy borrowers.[46] Such efforts to hide will be in vain. Because the criminal law and related sanctions are intruding everywhere, no one can adopt a philosophy of minding his own business and thereby avoid legal risk.

Combining this intrusiveness with the complexity and uncertainty of the legal requirements, and with the lack of any necessary relationship between criminal conviction and moral turpitude, people who get caught up by the legal system are angry, not repentant. There is grim humor in a paper prepared by a criminologist for a legal education seminar.[47] The author notes the difficulties of working with white-collar criminals: "Most of these clients have been upstanding citizens, have been involved in charities and community causes, and generally will have tremendous difficulty identifying with the reality of being charged with a criminal offense. The client may be indignant, even outraged, that he is being investigated, and he will often want to make this known." The lawyer's goal must be to keep the client from "transmitting a negative initial impression to the court." The article moves on to advice on dealing with the probation officer, who has the power to make or break the client. "The client must take responsibility for his actions. He must also provide a sense of how he feels about the offense, for example, remorse for transgressions, concern for victims if applicable. There should not be any excuses made. All too often, the defendant wants to explain how he is not really guilty, but had no choice except to take the deal offered by the government." Such remarks increase the likelihood of a stiff penalty or sentence.

This is solid advice. Quite a few defendants in wetlands cases would agree that protesting one's innocence or the unfairness of the system only makes matters worse. One of the defendants in *Weitzenhoff* also would agree. He denied his guilt on the witness stand, and his sentence was adjusted upward. Those convicted of a crime when they honestly tried to comply with the law or when they did not know that such a law existed find it difficult to grovel. One is left wondering how many of the 3,700 S&L executives in jail were sent there because they refused to admit wrongdoing.

Diminished Constitutional Protections

The continuing expansion in the ambit of the punitive system has been accompanied by a continuing decline in the scope of constitutional protections. As Timothy Lynch of the Cato Institute has analyzed in "Polluting Our Principles: Environmental Prosecutions and the Bill of Rights" (see Chapter 3), protections against warrantless searches, self-incrimination, right to counsel, and double jeopardy all have been seriously diluted.[48] An additional factor, not covered by Lynch, is that the standards of which information rises to the level of legal "evidence" are also being weakened.

The rules of evidence are primarily statutory or common law. Nonetheless, constitutional rights are involved, such as the rights to a public trial, to know the evidence against you, and to confront your accusers. There is also a right, which probably rises to constitutional stature, to be convicted only on the basis of competent evidence. For example, if a state decided to start sending people to jail on the basis of testimony from the Psychic Friends Network, one would hope such efforts would fail on constitutional grounds.

This right to be convicted only on the basis of competent evidence is also under attack. Much of the material on which regulations are based is junk science. But once in place, these rules have the same force as those based on the most well-established scientific truth. The rules governing wetlands and habitat protection for endangered species are particular examples, but there are many more.[49]

The decline in standards of evidence also leads directly to financial ruin. Refuting a junk science case is extraordinarily expensive. One must hire all kinds of experts and, in essence, reinvent the 1,000-year development of the scientific method in simple terms that a nontechnical jury can understand. This is very expensive.

The EPA is taking the dilution of evidentiary standards even further. In 1997 it issued a rule stating that under the Clean Air Act emitters can be convicted not only if the formal reference tests show that emissions exceeded the limits but also on the basis of "engineering calculations, indirect estimates of emissions, and direct measurement of emissions by a variety of means."[50] The exact meaning and import are not clear, but the ability to use "indirect estimates" as reliable evidence on which to convict is ominous.

Consequences of the Trend

The point of this article is not to argue that all regulations or sanctions are mistaken. There is much bad behavior in the world, and society must combat it. There is also a general consensus on the need to protect the environment, and an increasing tendency to judge harshly those who pollute the national commons of the air, land, and water.

Even accepting all this, the rush to punishment is imposing tremendous costs. The sheer number of sanctions, their shotgun character, their breadth and vagueness, the irrelevance of intent, the use of punishment as a first resort rather than a last resort, the failure to examine the moral nature of the conduct that is criminalized, and the strong overlay of zealotry are creating serious problems. Among these are economic damage, pervasive injustice, decline in respect for the law, and a sapping of the moral legitimacy of the government. These consequences are serious, and supporters of punitive measures should harken to more advice from Friedrich Nietzsche: "Whoever fights monsters should see to it that in the process he does not become a monster."[51]

Economic Effects

Concern about the economic impact of the current regulatory system does not require automatic opposition to anything that raises business costs. No one wants the United States to look like Eastern Europe, and in a world with an expanding population, the costs of protecting the environment must increase. But society must be concerned with obtaining as much value as possible for the costs incurred. Excessive reliance on punitive measures thwarts this objective and damages other important economic goals and interests.

The starting point for understanding the economics of the trend toward criminalization is to revisit the moral basis of classic criminal law. As long as the requirements of the criminal code are roughly congruent with the basic morality of society, people have the information they need to conform to it. They may not know the difference between first- and second-degree murder or the fine distinctions among forms of larceny, but they know that if they kill, steal, set fire to things, or do any of the other acts that their parents told them were wrong, they are likely to get in trouble. From an economic point of view, they have most of the information they need to obey the law, simply as a result of living in a society. This lowers the information costs of obedience.

People do not have the information they need to conform to the current regulatory scheme with its technical complexity, ambiguity, and, often, politically determined provisions. Further, given the irrelevance of intent, lack of information does not shield one from prosecution. This raises the costs of obedience extraordinarily. If even a finely tuned sense of right and wrong is an inadequate guide, then everyone must devote time and effort to ascertaining the law and the regulations and the cases and the interpretative letters and the agency's internal guidance. The high information costs burden even large firms, and can be prohibitive for small firms and individuals. Determining the requirements usually takes expensive analysis, and many issues are so complicated as to be indeterminable. Legal errors are common, and the enforcers might regard following erroneous advice not as an indication of good faith but rather as an attempt to fool the government. Errors of understanding also may lead a firm to spend large sums to prevent action that is, in fact, legal.

Unless a settled answer is readily available from an agency hot line, seeking clarification from the government is often futile and almost always slow. Solving a new problem requires a policy decision, and this is low on the agency priority list. After all, in the government's view, the supplicant has an easy out—assume that whatever it wants to do is illegal and refrain from doing it. That this option might be expensive, inconvenient, or impossible matters little. Systems for coordinating the mass of regulatory information are primitive, and only recently have many of the interpretative documents even become publicly accessible. Turnover of agency staff is constant, at a high price to institutional memory and continuity. Any lawyer who has worked on a problem for a client over time will testify that each visit to the agency probably will involve a new cast of characters. Each time, the new group is unfamiliar with the problem, having never seen the papers submitted to the last group. These papers must all be updated and resubmitted, and, with luck, one substantive discussion will be had before the cast changes again.

Knowledge costs are only one hurdle. If permits are needed, and they can number in the dozens, obtaining them is a serious expense and cause of delay. Proceeding without the permits is, of course, a serious offense, even if all actions taken are reasonable.

Resource requirements are also formidable. That pollution reduction takes money is not in itself a problem. The national consensus is that using the environment as a sewer is no longer acceptable. Compelling compliance by a system of punitive sanctions, however, creates enormous inefficiencies. To call something criminal, or even to respond to it with inordinate civil penalties, means that it is to be avoided, no matter what the cost. It is axiomatic that chasing zero risk in the face of diminishing marginal returns is enormously expensive. Further, it can make the resources required theoretically infinite because even if emissions are reduced to zero there is always a chance of error or breakdown, and avoiding this chance justifies commitment of yet more resources.

Emissions result from industrial processes that are subject to variation and upset. The EPA sometimes takes this variability into account in setting standards. For example, standards for treating hazardous waste are set at a level that can be met by a designated technology 95 percent of the time, meaning that facilities will fail to meet the standard 5 percent of the time. However, if the standard is enforced with criminal sanctions, then in practice the treatment must ensure that *no* exceedences occur. A standard reasonable at a 95 percent level of achievement can be impossible or exorbitantly expensive if it requires 100 percent certainty.

Any system that requires zero risk will become a voracious consumer of resources. Environmental protection must compete with other valued goals or objectives such as health care, employment, or general economic well-being. Resources are finite, and decisions about appropriate tradeoffs among their uses should involve comparisons at the margin. We must make a determination of how much incremental environmental protection is worth versus how much loss of other values is appropriate. The use of punitive sanctions prevents desirable tradeoffs. It decrees that any amount of environmental protection, no matter how small, is worth any amount of the sacrificed value, no matter how large. If numerous other areas of national policy are asserting the same absolute priority at the same time, through the use of punitive sanctions of their own, the whole system becomes a creaking structure of conflicting absolutist requirements.

In many cases, the increment of environmental protection that is to be purchased without regard for costs is small indeed. In *General Electric v. EPA*, the agency fined the company for a practice that saved money and reduced pollution. In *Weitzenhoff*, the defendants were trying to keep the sanitation system of the city of Honolulu functioning, and in the process they discharged 436,000 pounds of sewage over a period of 14 months when their permit allowed them to discharge only 409,000 pounds—a difference of roughly 6 percent. They went to jail. John Pozgai went to jail for placing fill on a "wetland"—actually a waterlogged vacant lot—that he himself had cleared of old tires, rusty metal, and other debris. One is hard-pressed to find any environmental benefit from these prosecutions; indeed, the reverse is true. Yet their effect will be to compel heavy spending by other entities on similarly pointless or destructive acts in tens of thousands of similar situations. Superfund is compelling the expenditure of billions of dollars for cleaning up hazardous waste at sites that no one intends to use. The program adds limited or negative economic value to the nation, but it is enforced with all the power of our punitive apparatus.[52]

To some degree, agencies try to deal with these problems through enforcement policy. They assert that as long as people are acting reasonably, they are in no real jeopardy. Experience does not bear this out, since many who appear to have been acting totally reasonably have been hit with stiff fines and sentences. Reasonableness is in the eye of the beholder. Some regulators and members of the environmental movement regard virtually any productive use of land as harmful and evil. If this view is the standard by which reasonableness is measured, it is difficult for someone who does not share this mind-set to act "reasonably."

Even if enforcement policy fulfilled an ideal of complete fairness, the problems facing any organization would not dissolve. Any corporate executive needs to know that his organization is in compliance, not that it is out of compliance but the agency will probably not treat the matter seriously. Agency emphasis on vicarious liability multiplies the importance of this certainty, precisely as the government intends. Even if management were willing to live with ambiguity, uncertainty creates impossible problems of internal administrative control. A large organization cannot develop guidelines about which rules will be enforced and which winked at; it must comply with all of them.

As an economic system, punitive sanctions represent the ultimate in command-and-control, and, as the Soviet experience should have taught us, omnipresent command-and-control is a poor way to run a country. Society wants its economic actors to proceed with intelligent discretion, balancing costs and benefits. Criminalization destroys this balance by declaring that all mistakes are intolerable and by removing all discretion to act reasonably under unforeseen circumstances. It also subjects all economic activity to the control of a regulatory *nomenklatura* that is every bit as unqualified to manage industrial and business activities as was its Soviet namesake.

The effect will be to undermine the dynamism and efficiency of all industries touched by the system. One of the great strengths of the U.S. economy has always been the freedom to act fostered by the common law system. Under this regime, people go through life trying to act reasonably, ethically, and with reasonable care. If someone fails on any of these counts, and someone else is injured as a result, the actor pays for the actual damage, but no more. There is no financial bonanza for the injured party or the government. Ultimate decisions are in the hands of independent judges, who have no vested interest in a particular program. This approach has served us well. It has encouraged entrepreneurial activism and responsibility. It is, in the current jargon, empowering.

The new emphasis on criminalization is the opposite. It dictates passivity, as clarification of the rules must be sought and prior approval secured. The consequences of an error bear no relation to the harm caused, or even to a determination that harm actually occurred. The approach is disempowering because it forces private actors to play "Mother, May I?" with the government over each minute aspect of their businesses.

The system of punitive enforcement badly serves the nation's goal of improving our international competitiveness. Environmentalists fear that other nations will obtain competitive advantage by means of a willingness to degrade their environments. This may be cause for concern, but another fear is far more immediate. Nations can compete by developing more efficient systems for promoting their social and environmental goals. The U.S. system uses multiple governments and agencies to enforce uncertain and sometimes inconsistent punitive standards, with no tolerance of error, and with each program asserting an absolute priority over all others. Any problems are to be solved by uncoordinated exercises of discretion by prosecutors.

To appreciate the full impact of the system we are creating, imagine it transferred to the area of automobile accidents. Everyone would agree that accidents are a bad thing. They cause personal injury and property damage, and they produce no economic benefit. If we apply the philosophy we are adopting in other areas, the answer is simple. We will outlaw accidents. From now on, it is a criminal offense to be involved in an auto accident. If some fuss-budget protests that people do not intend to have accidents, the answer is that they intend to drive cars and that they know that cars are sometimes in accidents. Therefore, they have all the intent that is necessary. They drive knowing that accidents are possible, just as industrial companies know that pollution is possible. Of course, since prosecutors may not want to take charge of all cases, we will also set up an accident agency and give it power to levy civil penalties and other sanctions on people who are involved in accidents. Further, all penalties will apply to all accidents, from the most minor fender bender to a multifatality interstate pileup. If you only bend a fender but the prosecutor thinks you are a bad guy, you can go to jail. (Unless, of course, you want to make a large contribution to a new program of Special Highway Projects that pays for extra guardrails, driver training, and so on.)

This system would reduce accidents. People facing stiff sentences regardless of fault or harm would modify their behavior. They would drive only when absolutely necessary, go 25 miles an hour on inter-state highways, stop even at green lights, and so on. So why don't we do this? Because we do not want to devote all of our energies and all of our resources to the single goal of avoiding all auto accidents. Yet, in other areas, that is precisely the standard we are adopting—that some single-minded goal must be pursued regard-less of any countervailing factors, goals, or costs.

Moral Impacts

The argument against excessive use of punitive measures is not solely an economic one. The same factors that make a punitive regime economically inefficient render it ethically deficient.

First, excessive reliance on punishment can increase harm. Because the regulated community must put its resources into averting any possible risk of violation, any area not covered by a rule is ignored. Resources go to reducing already trivial risks while more severe problems go unattended. A joint study of a refinery performed by a large oil company and the EPA found that the company could reduce overall risks substantially by de-emphasizing some risks now subject to regulation and diverting the saved resources to risks that are now uncontrolled.[53] The study has resulted in many speeches, but minimal action.

Unfairness to individuals is also growing and festering. Uncertainty in the law puts people at risk when engaging in normal but important economic activities. There is tremendous potential for results that offend the sense of justice. For example, should owners of businesses or corporate employees be jailed or fined because they did not simply go out of business rather than run the slightest risk of violating an ambiguous regulation? Regulations not tailored to a specific situation also create questions of fairness.

Ethical concerns are heightened by the reality that even an acute sense of morality is a poor guide to the New Criminalization. No one would defend the morality of most conduct that historically has been criminalized, or worry much about people who try to cut it close to the line. But for much of the New Criminalization, moral consensus exists only at a high level of generality. Our contemporary sensibilities do indeed condemn those who use the environment as a sewer for hazardous materials; discriminate on the grounds of race, gender, or physical characteristics; or cheat shareholders. But moral consensus at this level of generality is far more easily attained than consensus at a finer level of detail. The immorality of dumping chemicals indiscriminately does not tell one that dirt contaminated with pesticide is hazardous waste if the pesticide was spilled but not if it was applied deliberately. The need to avoid polluting the air does not tell one to use a sulfur scrubber even when burning nonsulfur coal. Ethical opposition to "discrimination" moves onto treacherous moral terrain when "nondiscrimination" comes to be defined as imposing affirmative action quotas or reconstructing a small business to provide better access or forbidding insurance premiums based on actual risk factors. A recent book on the explosion in employment litigation describes in detail how a system of legal controls can, using the sanctions of extraordinary damages, become unhinged from normal standards of behavior, economic efficiency, morality, and common sense.[54]

The capture of vast parts of the regulatory process by special interests adds a new dimension to these ethical issues. Take just one example out of thousands: It is a criminal act, a felony, to install a toilet that uses 3.5 gallons of water per flush. One must install a new

1.6-gallon model, a requirement foisted on America by an alliance of environmentalists and plumbing appliance manufacturers. Many people have aesthetic objections to the new models. Further, the value of the new model is small. In Washington, D.C., water costs $0.00383 per gallon. It would take 137 flushes to save a single dollar's worth of water. Heaven knows how long it would take to save enough on water bills to offset the cost of the newly mandated toilets. Financially beleaguered New York City spent $270 million paying property owners $240 each to tear out and replace old toilets. Unfortunately, some of the new models are inferior. They back up and become clogged more easily and must be flushed multiple times, so they use more water rather than less.[55]

What moral right does the government have to declare people criminals because they choose to spend a little more on water or because they have an aversion to clogged toilets? If water is scarce, then raise the price and let people make their own decisions on the basis of new information. In fact, the more one delves into the facts, the worse the government's moral position becomes. In the arid West, some farmers pay $7 per acre-foot for water. This could mean that water is not scarce. It could also mean that these farmers get water so inexpensively because they have political clout. So the government is making you a criminal if you fail to save tiny amounts of water that will then be given away to the politically powerful. A final irony is that these same farmers must also buy new-model toilets.

The toilet example strikes everyone as humorous, especially headline writers, who produced such tags as "A Whole New Bowl Game; Saying No to 'Low-Flow,' Buyers Flush Out Old Toilets."[56] However, the principle involved is not at all funny. Nor is the effect on the nation when the example is multiplied by the several hundred thousand regulations in effect. With every flush of a new-model toilet, some of the moral legitimacy and credibility of the legal system and the government goes down the drain. If the criminal law is so absurdly applied to new toilets, why should anyone believe the government when warned that freon must be outlawed for the sake of the ozone layer or energy use must be curtailed to prevent global warming or development of property must be stopped for the sake of endangered species? Simply put, when government criminalizes almost everything, it also trivializes the very concept of criminality.

The capture of chunks of the regulatory system by various special interests leads to a loss of moral legitimacy for another reason. It causes particular activities to be criminalized precisely *because* of the lack of community moral consensus. The heavy hand of government regulation is used to compensate for the lack of pressure from society or internal conscience. This technique has its uses; it can sway people who are on the fence. But the fact that something is a good idea in one context does not make it good in every situation, and the technique first wears out, then backfires, when overused.

Many landowners are morally outraged by the draconian application of wetlands regulation, which has turned into a large-scale program of property appropriation. They also know that the program was never explicitly passed by Congress. It was created by regulators, who were pushed by activist judges and crafty drafters of legislative history. Hence, its moral legitimacy is thin. Violations are criminalized precisely for the *in terrorem* effect because the law does not correspond with the people's sense of moral right. It is somewhat similar to an occupying army shooting a hostage occasionally to instill fearful obedience from the populace.

The federal budget crunch is making this problem worse. As Congress loses the financial freedom to give money to favored constituencies, it passes laws forcing private actors to transfer wealth to them. Because these laws are perceived as lacking moral legitimacy, they require constant escalation of the effort to enforce them. Also, if money for enforcement is limited, agencies have strong incentives to impose disproportionate costs on the private sector to relieve the pressure on their own budgets. For example, the EPA may require expensive air-monitoring technology to save itself trivial expenditures on inspection. Agencies may also become more punitive. If a few violators can be prosecuted, the temptation to make horrible examples of those few is overwhelming.

Overuse of punitive sanctions damages the moral fabric of the culture. By lumping trivial with serious transgressions, it undermines the people's sense of moral priorities. In addition, when people who regard themselves as responsible moral actors learn that they have committed criminal offenses that they have never even heard of, their first reaction is disbelief. Their second is contempt for the law. The developing perception is that one cannot possibly keep up with all the rules and cannot afford to try. The rational person must shrug and accept the possibility of criminal conviction as one of the risks of life, like automobile accidents or rare diseases— doing what is reasonable to avoid troubles but recognizing that no one is immune to chance.

The moral fabric of the culture will be undermined in another way—corruption. The lack of clarity in the laws and the immense bureaucratic discretion to define standards create serious risks of corruption even if the stakes are purely economic. The addition of punitive sanctions raises the stakes, and over time levels of bribery and extortion will rise. This will provide new business opportunities for those particularly skilled in these arts.

Even without corruption, many of the new sanctions lend themselves to unfortunate enforcement tactics. Allegations that forfeitures of property are the snake pit of law enforcement are becoming louder. Some local officials have effectively made such laws vehicles for theft of other people's property.[57]

The power of prosecutors is also exploding. Even when law enforcement is at its best, prosecution must be selective; not enough resources exist to pursue everyone. So how are the sacrifices chosen? Some of it is chance, such as public notice. Some targets are chosen for tactical reasons, to impress other potential targets. Some targeting is big game hunting and political ambition. And is there any real doubt that some large political contributors are buying insulation from enforcement excess?

Another good way to become a target is to look as if you can turn in someone more interesting. If you can, you get a deal; if you cannot, that is your misfortune. When every minor violation is criminal, such as an error in filling out a form, prosecutors find this technique easy to use. The pressures for perjury are obvious.

Public awareness of these issues creates an impression that enforcement is increasingly political and tendentious. True or not, the perception is damaging public respect for the legal and law enforcement systems, which is already low. Indisputably, the increase in criminalization has turned tremendous power over to the discretion of enforcers, a development deeply alien to traditional, and well-founded, American skepticism of untrammeled authority. This shift is accentuated by new sentencing guidelines that restrict a judge's freedom to reduce a sentence in light of special circumstances. Combine this limit on judicial mercy with a regulatory system so extensive and complex as to make anyone chargeable, and government by prosecutorial discretion is complete.

Conclusions

The often quoted (and always taken out of context) cure comes to mind: "[F]irst . . . let's kill all the lawyers." The legal profession is, indeed, a primary villain. Its "there oughta be a law" mindset has encouraged government to react to every perceived problem with a new penalty, and to respond to each failure of this approach by making the penalty more severe and redoubling enforcement efforts. This is a destructive cycle.

The late Paul Bator, a thoughtful scholar of the legal system, criticized both the courts and the nation's legal elites for failing "in their essential professional tasks of stabilizing, clarifying, and improving the national law, so as to make it useful for its 'consumers'," and for their lack of "a sense of decent obligation to [those who must use, obey, and apply the law]."[58] The criticism is well-deserved.

A succession of congressmen, presidents, state legislators, and governors also deserves censure. During the past 25 years, the habit of loading criminal provisions and other sanctions into every law has become a thoughtless reflex. No consideration is given to the problems discussed here. And at the federal level, neither legislators nor presidents have made any serious effort to rein in regulators who use vague statutes backed up by hair-raising penalties to stretch their authority to the utmost. The congressional charade of railing against "out-of-control bureaucrats" one day and giving them more money and power the next has become a tiresome act.

The process also feeds on itself. Laws based on raw political power or campaign contributions rather than on a shared sense of morality lack legitimacy. Such commandments are likely to be violated whenever people think they can get away with it. This does indeed increase the level of "criminality" in society, and creates a need for more enforcement and harsher penalties.

The courts also deserve censure. With a few notable exceptions judges have spent the past 20 years not noticing the erosion of many constitutional and common law protections. Basic doctrines of administrative law, including presumptions of agency competence and good faith, were formulated in the very different environment of the 1930s. Every other intellectual discipline that studies government has gone through a revolution since then—not the law. Its assumptions are those of the Progressive Era of 1900 to 1920, the New Deal of the 1930s, and the Great Society of the 1960s. In this view, Congress, or state legislatures, enact vague laws to promote the public interest. They then delegate implementation of these laws to administrative agencies and hope that they act as wise guardians and disinterested experts bringing to bear the best in technical knowledge to achieve some social optimum. Courts have been heavy on presumptions of regularity and constitutionality, on deference to agency expertise, and on the gospel that all government officials operate in disinterested good faith. It is a smiley-face view of things, and it bears little resemblance to the harder, messier world of contemporary legal and political analysis.

The first step toward reform is educational and political. Since virtually everyone is affected by these issues, virtually everyone needs to become informed and motivated to act. Members of all three branches of government need to be pounded with the message that the present trend is wrong, that it is harming society, and that it is eroding trust in, and respect for, government and law. Business organizations need to devote particular effort to this. They are on the sharp edge, but seem paralyzed by the public relations problems that might be created by any action that could be interpreted as trying to defend "criminal" conduct.

Political conservatives bear a particular burden. They need to reenergize their fight to convince people that the role of government must shrink because government intervention in any area will almost certainly lead not just to economic inefficiency, but also to an expansion of the criminal code and a delegitimizing of law, all of which damages society.

Leaving aside fights over the basic role of government, there is a second line of defense. Where the government must act, serious attention needs to be devoted to developing alternatives to command-and-control regulation, such as the development of markets. Punitive sanctions are the inevitable tool of any system of command-and-control. Therefore, the fight for alternative approaches is a high-stakes game.

Those who favor a more limited role for government also must pay attention to the problems of the civil justice system. Many businesses complain about the heavy random risks the system now imposes on them. At least part of this trend is due to the difficulty of getting rapid, efficient, and fair resolution of disputes. If civil justice were swifter, more consistent, and better, there would be less pressure to convert commercial disputes into RICO violations or to pile up punitive damage provisions or to substitute environmental regulations for private nuisance actions. Reforming civil justice would create possibilities for limiting the New Criminalization in favor of a system designed around the common law virtues.

At a more specific level, a number of reforms are needed:

- An obvious measure is for Congress to review the penalty policies in every program and provide clear guidelines and limitations or to require the administering agency to do it with active congressional oversight.

- Another step is to reinstate intent as an important element of an offense, possibly by resurrecting the old concepts of *malum in se*, *mens rea*, and *malum prohibitum*. Ignorance of the law should often be an excuse, and concepts of fair notice should be expanded to meet the realities of the modern world. Rules that are not ascertainable after reasonable effort should be enforced only by a cease-and-desist order, not by civil or criminal penalties. Even beyond this, there should be an explicit defense of acting reasonably under the circumstances, regardless of whether formal commands were violated, and this should be adjudged by some authority other than the implementing agency.

- Courts should be more protective of common law rights and constitutional principles. Old concepts of vagueness and undue delegation, now in desuetude, should be revived. An overly activist judiciary is rightly to be feared, but the opposite sin of paralysis is equally grievous. Substituting judicial whim for the judgment of the political organs is a bad thing, but this can be distinguished from insisting that those organs meet reasonable standards of clarity and competence. The courts need to develop a jurisprudence suited to the regulatory state as it has developed during the past half century, and to their own role as a backup quality controller if the other branches refuse to exercise the function over their own activities.[59]

The criminalization of highly complex and often conflicting regulations with virtually no requirement of intent leads to situations in which even the well educated and well informed cannot be sure what the law is and what they must do to comply with it. If Congress will exercise the legislative authority and oversight responsibility granted it, and if courts will reinvigorate common law principles and again require intent to be proven before allowing the imposition of criminal sanctions or quasi-criminal penalties, we will experience a sea change. From a regulatory perspective, those things that society collectively agrees should be regulated will continue to be regulated, with regulators focusing on the real harms to society. From an economic perspective, we will see greater efficiency with resources being devoted not only to a cleaner environment but also to other productive uses. From a moral perspective, law-abiding citizens will not live in fear of mistakenly violating an obscure regulation. From a constitutional perspective, those accused of regulatory crimes will enjoy the same safeguards as those accused of traditional crimes. And finally, from a political perspective, cynicism will recede, and the government's legitimacy in the eyes of the populace will increase substantially.

This is an abridged version of a monograph originally published by the National Legal Center for the Public Interest, June 1997.

Notes

1. Quoted in Bartlett's *Familiar Quotations, Thus Spake Zarathustra*, pt. II, ch. 29, 1992, 16th ed., p. 552.

2. Richard J. Lazarus, "Meeting the Demands of Integration in the Evolution of Environmental Law: Reforming Environmental Criminal Law," *Georgetown Law Journal* 83, (1995): 2407, 2441–42.

3. John F. Cooney et al., "Criminal Enforcement of Environmental Laws," in *Environmental Law Institute, Environmental Crimes Deskbook* 5 (1996): 8 [hereinafter "Criminal Enforcement"].

4. Lazarus, see n. 2, p. 2408, n. 4.

5. Timothy Lynch, "Polluting Our Principles: Environmental Prosecutions and the Bill of Rights," Cato Institute Policy Analysis no. 223, April 20, 1995.

6. Rick Henderson, "Crimes Against Nature," *Reason*, December 1993, pp. 18, 21.

7. Robert H. Fuhrman, "Improving EPA's Civil Penalty Policies—And Its Not-So-Gentle BEN Model," *Environment Reporter* (BNA) (September 9, 1994): 874.

8. *FY95: EPA, FY 1995 Enforcement and Compliance Assurance Accomplishments Report* 3–4 (July 1996); FY96: "EPA Set Record in '96 of 262 Criminal Cases on Pollution Charges," *Wall Street Journal*, February 26, 1997, p. B5.

9. *United States v. Mills*, 817 F. Supp. 1546 (N.D. Fla. 1992).

10. This story has been widely recounted. See, for example, Max Boot, "The Wetlands Gestapo," *Wall Street Journal*, March 3, 1997, p. A18.

11. See, for example, Dale French, "Adirondack Couple Faces 50 Years in Prison for Leaky Septic System," *Land Rights Letter*, p. 1 (December 1996); John Fulton Lewis, " 'Duell' Objectives: Criminalizing Civil Law & 'Gutting' the Opposition" (Part 1), *Land Rights Letter*, p. 1 (January/February 1997). I have called the New York State Department of Environmental Conservation three times about this case. Each time, I have left a message saying that these facts are being reported by property rights advocacy groups and that I would like to hear the state's side of the matter. I have yet to receive a return telephone call.

12. Elyse Tanouye, "SmithKline to Pay $325 Million to Settle Federal Claims of Lab-Billing Fraud," *Wall Street Journal*, February 25, 1997, p. B6; "SmithKline Beecham Settles Medicare Dispute for $325 Million," February 24, 1997 (SmithKline Beecham Press Release).

13. Robert A. Rosenblatt, "Government Auditors Question Medicare for Long-Term Hospice Care," *Washington Post*, March 16, 1997, p. A17.

14. Ralph K. Winter, "Paying Lawyers, Empowering Prosecutors, and Protecting Managers: Raising the Cost of Capital in America," *Duke Law Journal* 42 (1993): 945, 955.

15. Holman W. Jenkins Jr., "Will the Real S&L 'Crooks' Please Stand Up?" *Wall Street Journal*, October 1, 1996, p. A23.

16. John E. Yang, "Hyde's Denial Led to Separate S&L Settlement; Lawmaker Won't Pay in $850,000 Deal," *Washington Post*, February 24, 1997, p. A4.

17. See "Pennsylvania Agency Sues Morgan, Lewis over Failed Insurers," *Wall Street Journal*, February 28, 1997, p. B3; Winter, see n. 15, p. 961. See also *The RICO Racket*, ed. Gary McDowell (Washington: National Legal Center for the Public Interest, 1989).

18. Lazarus, see n. 2, pp. 2409–10, 2500–09.

19. Letter of May 20, 1987, from Jacqueline W. Sales, Chief Regulatory Development Section, (EPA), to Frank Czigler, Environmental Department (S&W Waste Inc. in New Jersey) (on file with author).

20. Margaret N. Strand, "Federal Wetlands Law," *Environmental Law Institute, Wetlands Desk Book* 3 (1993): 17.

21. Roger Marzulla, "Presumed Guilty: Wetlands Criminal Prosecutions," *Farmers, Ranchers and Environmental Law* 39 (1995): 41, 72 (Washington: National Legal Center for the Public Interest).

22. James V. DeLong, *Property Matters: How Property Rights Are under Assault—and Why You Should Care* (New York: Free Press, 1997) p. 134.

23. Lazarus, see n. 2, pp. 2428–41.

24. 438 U.S. 422 (1971).

25. *United States v. Staples*, 114 S. Ct. 1793 (1994) (footnotes omitted).

26. Ibid. at 1805:

> Some Courts of Appeals have adopted a variant of the third reading, holding that the Government must show that the defendant knew the gun was a machine gun, but allowing inference of the requisite knowledge where a visual inspection of the gun would reveal that it has been converted into an automatic weapon. See *United States v. O'Mara*, 963 F.2d 1288, 1291 (CA9 1992); *United States v. Anderson*, 885 F.2d 1248, 1251 (CA5 1989) (en banc).

27. The others were *Ratzlaf v. United States*, 114 S. Ct. 655 (1994) (government must show that defendant knew that structuring cash withdrawals so as to avoid a bank's

reporting requirements was illegal); *Posters 'N' Things Ltd. v. United States*, 114 S. Ct. 1793 (1994) (government must show that defendant knew that items sold were likely to be used with illegal drugs and that it knowingly made use of an interstate conveyance); *United States v. X-Citement Video*, 115 S. Ct. 464 (1994) (government must show that defendant knew that the performer in a sexually explicit videotape was a minor).

28. 101 F.3d 386 (5th Cir. 1996).

29. 1 F.3d 1523, *amended on denial of rehearing and rehearing en banc*, 35 F.3d 1275 (9th Cir. 1994), *cert. denied*, 115 S. Ct. 939 (1995).

30. Alexander Volokh and Roger Marzulla, "Environmental Enforcement: In Search of Both Effectiveness and Fairness," Reason Foundation, Policy Study No. 210, August 1996, p. 6.

31. For a discussion of this line of cases, see Margaret N. Strand, "The 'Regulatory Confusion' Defense to Environmental Penalties: Can You Beat the Rap?" *Environmental Law Report* 22 (Washington, Environmental Law Institute; 1992): 10330.

32. 937 F.2d 649 (D. C. Cir. 1991).

33. 53 F.3d 1324 (D.C. Cir. 1995).

34. Ibid.

35. See Lazarus, n. 2, pp. 2476–84.

36. 35 F.3d at 1298.

37. "Criminal Enforcement," see n. 3, pp. 12–19.

38. Ibid., p. 13 (citing EPA memoranda).

39. *Hearings on S. 851, The Wetlands Regulatory Reform Act of 1995 Before the Senate Committee on Public Works*, 104th Cong., 1st Sess. 9–11 (November 1, 1995) (statement of James S. Burling).

40. Brief for the Appellant, *United States v. Wilson*, No. 96-4498(L) (4th Cir. 1996).

41. EPA, *FY 1995 Enforcement and Compliance Assurance Accomplishments Report 3–13* (July 1996).

42. Lynch, see n. 5, p. 8.

43. Telephone interview with Thomas Adams (February 1, 1997).

44. "Criminal Enforcement," see n. 3, p. 33.

45. See, for example, Jonathan M. Moses, "U.S. Presses Firms to Stop Supporting Accused Aides," *Wall Street Journal*, November 4, 1993, p. B1.

46. Timothy Ryan, "Banking's New Risk—Litigation," *Wall Street Journal*, November 13, 1992, p. A14.

47. Sheila Balkan, "Preparing the Business Client for Criminal Proceedings," ABA Section of Litigation, Paper No. 531-0023/5H, November 1993.

48. Cato Institute Policy Analysis no. 223, April 20, 1995; see also, Timothy Lynch, "Dereliction of Duty: The Constitutional Record of President Clinton" Cato Institute Policy Analysis no. 271, March 31, 1997, www.cato.org.

49. Michael H. Levin, "EPA'S Indefensible 'Credible Evidence' Rule: A Critical Analysis," Washington Legal Foundation Working Paper No. 76, 1997; *Junk Science Home Page*, www.junkscience.com.

50. EPA, "Final Rule: Credible Evidence Revisions," *Federal Register* 62 (February 24, 1997): 8313.

51. Quoted in Bartlett's *Familiar Quotations, Thus Spake Zarathustra*, pt. II, ch. 29, 1992, 16th ed., p. 552.

52. For an extensive analysis, see James V. DeLong, "Privatizing Superfund: How to Clean Up Hazardous Waste," Cato Institute Policy Analysis no. 247, December 18, 1995, www.cato.org.

53. Bill Mintz, "Yorktown: A Revolution in Regulation?" *Houston Chronicle*, March 13, 1994, p. F1.

54. Walter K. Olsen, *The Excuse Factory: How Employment Law Is Paralyzing the American Workplace* (New York: Free Press, 1997).

55. Clifford J. Levy, "Report Says Toilet Program Wasted Water and Money," *New York Times*, July 31, 1996, p. B3.

56. Tamara Jones, *Washington Post*, May 28, 1996, p. A1. The jump-page headline was "As Rules Take Effect, a Run on 3.5-Gallon Toilets." See also Cindy Skrzycki, "Going Against the Flow: One Legislator Isn't Bowled Over by a Conservation Rule," *Washington Post*, March 21, 1997, p. G3.

57. See DeLong, n. 22, pp. 275–77.

58. Paul M. Bator, "What Is Wrong with the Supreme Court?" *University of Pittsburgh Law Review* 51 (1990): 673, 674, 691.

59. See James V. DeLong, "New Wine for a New Bottle: Judicial Review in the Regulatory State," *Virginia Law Review* 72 (1986): 399.

3. Polluting Our Principles: Environmental Prosecutions and the Bill of Rights

Timothy Lynch

American lawmakers, spurred by their concern for the natural environment, have created a regulatory environment in which "the barriers of government are broken down and the boundaries of the Constitution defaced."[1] They seem to have lost sight of the importance of constitutional protections as they measure their accomplishments in terms of numbers of prosecutions and convictions and the dollar value of fines.[2] All three branches of government at both the federal and state levels have seriously eroded important protections, including the principle of "specificity" in penal statutes, the Fourth Amendment guarantee against unreasonable searches and seizures, the constitutional bar on double prosecutions, and the Fifth Amendment privilege against self-incrimination.

The Federalization and Criminalization of Environmental Law

The federal government did not enter the field of environmental law until 1890, largely because early Congresses and presidents harbored serious doubts as to whether the federal government had the constitutional authority to develop and regulate natural resources.[3] The scope of the first federal environmental statute, the Rivers and Harbors Act (1890), was so modest that the act passed without fanfare or controversy.[4] Indeed, the primary purpose of the statute had nothing to do with environmental protection. The act was meant to facilitate trade among the states by prohibiting commercial obstructions of navigable waterways. A tangential purpose of the statute was to prohibit pollution of navigable waters. The law was not controversial, because it merely supplemented the public nuisance laws of the states. Criminal prosecutions under the act were extremely rare. In fact, only 25 environmental crimes were prosecuted by the federal government before 1982.[5]

45

The federalization of environmental law began in earnest, on April 22, 1970, the first "Earth Day." A *New York Times* reporter compared it with Mother's Day because it was apparent that no one in public office could oppose it.[6]

Earth Day captured the imagination of federal lawmakers. Sen. Gaylord Nelson (D-Wis.) advocated a constitutional amendment that would empower the federal government to guarantee every American an "inalienable right to a decent environment," and former vice president Hubert H. Humphrey called on the United Nations to establish a global agency to "strengthen, enforce and monitor pollution abatement throughout the world."[7] Although decidedly less enthusiastic, Republican leaders also joined the movement for political action. Through a White House spokesperson, President Richard M. Nixon issued a statement saying that he hoped Earth Day would be the start of a continuing campaign against pollution. A few months later, in July 1970, President Nixon proposed the creation of a new federal regulatory body, the Environmental Protection Agency.

Since 1970 the federal government has dramatically expanded its regulatory and enforcement activity. Consider the rapid succession of events:

- In 1971 the EPA had about 7,000 employees and a budget of $700 million. By the mid-'90s the EPA had 17,600 employees and a budget of about $6 billion.[8]
- Many major environmental statutes were passed rapidly in the 1970s: the Clean Air Act (1970); the Ocean Dumping Act (1972); the Clean Water Act (1972); the Federal Insecticide, Fungicide, and Rodenticide Act (1972); the Endangered Species Act (1973); the Safe Drinking Water Act (1974); the Resource Conservation and Recovery Act (1976); and the Comprehensive Environmental Response, Compensation and Liability Act (1980).
- During the 1980s Congress systematically elevated environmental criminal violations from misdemeanors to felonies.[9]
- In 1981 the EPA created the Office of Criminal Enforcement. Within months, the Department of Justice created its own Environmental Crimes Unit in anticipation of case referrals from the EPA. Both units have grown steadily over the years. In 1982 the EPA had 21 criminal investigators. By 1992 the cadre had

grown to 60—and the Pollution Prosecution Act of 1990, which was signed by President George H. W. Bush, required the EPA to have at least 200 investigators by the end of 1995.[10]

- Enforcement figures have skyrocketed. From 1982 to 1996 the federal government secured more than 1,400 criminal indictments and more than 1,000 convictions.[11]

By 1990 a fully centralized command-and-control regulatory regime was firmly entrenched, and a frightening bureaucratic imperative has now taken over. Many businesses are operating in what is essentially a regulatory police state. An environmental law treatise published in 1994 acknowledges that "it is virtually impossible for a major company (or government facility) to be in complete compliance with all regulatory requirements. [And yet] virtually every instance of noncompliance can be readily translated into a [criminal] violation."[12] Environmental criminal prosecutions are increasingly the result of bad luck, not of blameworthy choice.

The most alarming aspect of environmental prosecutions is that businesspeople cannot avail themselves of many of the constitutional protections that are explicitly set forth in the Bill of Rights. Attorney Barry C. Groveman observes, "We are seeing a political climate of affirmative action on the environment in which a businessman does not have civil rights."[13] The lesson of history is that, in the long run, violations of civil liberties have no ideological pedigree. Thus, it is important that men and women of good will—conservatives, liberals, and others—be alarmed by the legal trends we are seeing today and act to check unconstitutional encroachment wherever it occurs.[14]

Vague Statutes: A Guessing Game for Business

The Fifth and Fourteenth Amendments to the Constitution guarantee that no American citizen can be deprived of "life, liberty, or property, without due process of law." The Supreme Court has held that "a statute which either forbids or requires the doing of an act in terms so vague that men of common intelligence must necessarily guess at its meaning and differ as to its application, violates the first essential of due process of law."[15] In recent years, however, the government has successfully limited the application of that principle in the context of "regulatory crimes." The explosion of vaguely written environmental rules has spawned a civil liability minefield for business. The criminalization of violations of those regulations is making the terrain so treacherous that even lawyers are having difficulty remaining on the right side of the law.[16]

From Caligula to John Marshall

History is filled with examples of tyrannical governments that were able to persecute unpopular groups and innocent individuals by keeping the law's requirements from the people. The Roman emperor Caligula, for example, posted new laws high on the columns of buildings so that they could not be studied by ordinary citizens. Such abominable policies were discarded during the Enlightenment, and a new set of principles—known generally as the "rule of law"— took hold. Included among those principles are the requirements of legality and specificity.

"Legality" means a regularized process, ideally rooted in moral principle, by which crimes are designated and prosecuted by government. The Enlightenment philosophy was expressed by the *maxim nullum crimen sine lege* (there is no crime without a law). In other words, persons can be punished only for conduct previously prohibited by law. That principle is clearly enunciated in the ex post facto clause of the U.S. Constitution (article I, section 9). Note, however, that the purpose of the ex post facto clause can be subverted if the legislature can pass a criminal law that condemns conduct in general terms—such as "seditious and treasonous" behavior. Such a law would not give individuals fair warning of the conduct prohibited. Thus, "specificity" requires that all penal statutes be drafted with precision. The specificity principle guards against arbitrary enforcement and gives individuals the opportunity to adjust their behavior to conform to the law's requirements.[17]

Although the ex post facto and due process clauses were intended to guard against legislative and prosecutorial abuses, the American judiciary recognized that judges were also capable of violating the principles embedded in those clauses. An expansive or unusual interpretation of a criminal statute, for example, could surprise a citizen who honestly believed his conduct to be lawful. In 1820 Chief Justice John Marshall warned, "It would be dangerous, indeed, to carry the principle, that a case that is within the reason or mischief of a statute, is within its provisions, so far as to punish a crime not enumerated in the statute, because it is of equal atrocity, or of kindred character, with those which are enumerated."[18] To guard against the injustice of unfair surprise, the courts have followed the "rule of lenity," which holds that any ambiguity concerning the scope of criminal statutes is to be resolved in the defendant's favor.

The principle of specificity operates together with the rule of lenity to advance two important values implicit in the concept of due process of law. First, they give every individual fair warning about conduct that is prohibited. Second, they reduce the likelihood of arbitrary and discriminatory application of the law by keeping policy matters away from policemen, administrative bureaucrats, prosecutors, judges, and juries, who would have to resolve ambiguities on an ad hoc, subjective basis.

Prosecutors Secure a "Regulatory" Exception

Although the specificity requirement remains a basic principle of criminal law, a "regulatory" exception has crept into modern jurisprudence. The Supreme Court allows "greater leeway" in regulatory matters because the practicalities of modern governance supposedly limit "the specificity with which legislators can spell out prohibitions."[19] Over the past 50 years, fuzzy regulatory terms such as "unreasonable," "unusual," and "excessive" have withstood constitutional challenge.

Not only has the rule of lenity been ignored in the context of regulatory offenses, it also has been turned on its head. When an ordinary criminal statute is ambiguous, the courts give the benefit of the doubt to the accused, but when a regulatory provision is ambiguous, the benefit of the doubt is given to the prosecutor.[20]

Environmental Laws That Lawyers Cannot Decipher

The modern Supreme Court precedents have allowed lawmakers at the federal and state levels to pass vague environmental legislation. In a 1993 survey by Arthur Andersen Environmental Services and the *National Law Journal*, 47 percent of 200 corporate attorneys interviewed said that the environmental duty that occupied most of their time and energy was trying to determine the seemingly basic question of whether or not their companies were complying with the law. The *Journal* reported, "Nearly 70 percent [of the attorneys surveyed] said they didn't believe total compliance with the law was achievable—due to the complexity of the law, the varying interpretations of regulators, the ever-present role of human error, and the cost."[21] Conscientious laypersons could try to interpret the regulations themselves, but such attempts are likely to lead to confusion and frustration. After all, if a federal judge found RCRA's provisions "mind-numbing," how can an ordinary businessperson possibly comprehend his legal rights and obligations?[22]

One explanation for the presence of so many vague rules in environmental law is the fact that the courts reward sloppy lawmaking by resolving ambiguities in the government's favor. As previously noted, the judiciary does not adhere to the rule of lenity in the regulatory context. When an ordinary criminal statute is unclear, the ambiguity is resolved in the defendant's favor, but in environmental prosecutions the government itself is the beneficiary of unclear provisions. In *United States v. Standard Oil* (1966), for example, the Supreme Court found the statutory term "refuse matter" to include commercially valuable gasoline.[23] That interpretation made it possible for the government to prosecute Standard Oil for an accidental oil spill under the Rivers and Harbors Act. Three justices dissented from that ruling because it ignored the "traditional canon that penal statute[s] . . . be narrowly construed."[24]

In *United States v. Phelps Dodge Corporation* (1975), a federal district court considered the scope of a provision of the Clean Water Act.[25] Phelps Dodge argued that the terms "navigable waters" and "waters of the United States" could not be fairly construed to encompass "normally dry arroyos through which water may flow."[26] Even though the court found the legal issue to be a "close" one, the prosecutor's expansive interpretation of the statute was upheld. The *Standard Oil* and *Phelps Dodge* precedents have encouraged environmental prosecutors to overreach with novel legal theories that would probably be considered abuse of process in ordinary criminal proceedings.[27] When the specificity principle and the rule of lenity are ignored, the dangers of arbitrary and discriminatory enforcement are heightened. Enforcement of environmental law is likely to be inconsistent and arbitrary because the prosecutor can pursue violations in one of three ways: (1) administratively, (2) civilly, or (3) criminally.[28]

Government officials assure the public that decisions to bring charges are made by disinterested attorneys who take all of the relevant information into account. Enforcement decisions are supposedly based on considered judgments of what will ultimately further the "public good." A critical examination of decisions to charge, however, would reveal that some prosecutors act in their own self-interest. It is no secret that many prosecutors harbor ambitions for higher office. Those individuals might allow factors such as public opinion and potential media coverage to affect their charging decisions. Although some offices follow strict guidelines that are based on objective criteria, other offices are guided by nothing more than the personal predilections of the attorney assigned to the case. A Los Angeles County prosecutor, for example, says the decision about whether to indict a company depends on how the violation affects his neck hairs. "When the little hairs on the back of your neck stand up, it's a felony. When it just makes you tingle, it's a misdemeanor. If it does nothing to you at all, it's a civil problem."[29] Those "criteria" are probably not representative of the ones used in the decisionmaking processes in government offices across the country, but they are a stark reminder of the abuse of power that is possible when the freedom and reputation of ordinary citizens rest on the "professional judgment" of a prosecutor.

The Framers of the Constitution understood that democracy alone was no guarantor of justice. As James Madison noted, "It will be of little avail to the people that the laws are made by men of their own choice if the laws be so voluminous that they cannot be read, or so incoherent that they cannot be understood; if they be repealed or revised before they are promulgated, or undergo such incessant changes that no man, who knows what the law is today, can guess what it will be tomorrow."[30] Unfortunately, Madison's nightmare of unbridled lawmaking is an apt description of environmental policy in the 1990s. The EPA, for example, received so many queries about the meaning of the Resource Conservation and Recovery Act that it set up a special hot line for RCRA questions. Note, however, that the "EPA itself does not guarantee that its answers are correct, and reliance on wrong information given over the RCRA hot line is no defense to an enforcement action."[31] The situation is so obviously rotten that many prosecutors are acknowledging that there is simply too much uncertainty in environmental law. Former Massachusetts attorney general Scott Harshbarger concedes, "One thing we haven't done well in government is make it very clear, with bright lines, what kinds of activity will subject you to . . . criminal or civil prosecution."[32]

51

The Supreme Court ought to revisit the precedents that created a regulatory exception to the requirement of specificity. Those precedents are making a mockery of the due process principles that have helped to secure procedural justice in ordinary criminal cases. The Court should also apply the rule of lenity to regulatory matters. Legal uncertainties ought to be resolved in favor of private individuals and organizations, not the state.

Warrantless and Unreasonable Searches

The Fourth Amendment provides that "The right of the people to be secure in their persons, houses, papers, and effects, against unreasonable searches and seizures, shall not be violated, and no warrants shall issue, but upon probable cause, supported by Oath or affirmation, and particularly describing the place to be searched, and the person or things to be seized."

The Colonial Experience

Although most Americans think of the amendment in the context of criminal proceedings, its function is far broader. "It serves as one the fundamental brakes on governmental intrusion into our lives."[33] As Judge E. Barrett Prettyman observed in 1949, "To say that a man suspected of a crime has a right to protection against search of his home without a warrant, but that a man not suspected of a crime has no such protection, is a fantastic absurdity.... To view the Amendment as a limitation upon an otherwise unlimited right of search is to invert completely the true posture of rights and the limitations thereon."[34]

Although the Supreme Court is often divided in Fourth Amendment cases, the governing principle of the vacillating precedents is that "a search of private property without consent is 'unreasonable' unless it has been authorized by a valid search warrant."[35] An important precedent was set, however, in *Davis v. United States* (1946).[36] In that case the Supreme Court upheld a governmental seizure of rationing coupons at a gasoline station. The decision was noteworthy because the majority opinion emphasized that the filling station was a place of business, not a private residence. The implication, of course, was that the holding might have been different if the seizure had taken place on noncommercial property.

After *Davis*, owners of commercial property began to receive less constitutional protection than owners of residential property. The legal trend was confirmed in *Donovan v. Dewey* (1981) in which the Supreme Court made explicit what had previously been only implied: Government has "greater latitude to conduct warrantless inspections of commercial property" than of residential property.[37] It was from that sort of reasoning that the "administrative search warrant" was born. According to a treatise on the Fourth Amendment, the probable cause standard for administrative searches "bears no resemblance to the usual requirements of probable cause in criminal procedure. Administrative search warrants may be issued solely on a showing that reasonable legislative or administrative standards for conducting an inspection are satisfied with respect to the particular place to be searched. There need be no probable cause that a violation has occurred or is occurring in a particular place."[38]

The Fourth Amendment guarantee was weakened again in the 1970s when the Supreme Court held that the business premises of certain "closely regulated" industries were exempt from the (already lax) rules concerning administrative searches. In *United States v. Biswell* (1972), the Court considered the constitutionality of a gun control law that authorized federal agents to inspect the premises of federally licensed gun dealers without an administrative warrant.[39] The Court upheld the law because the pervasive regulations governing firearms essentially put those engaged in the business on notice as to the government's powers. The majority opinion suggested that if the "threat to privacy" were to reach "impressive dimensions," the Court might be inclined to revisit the issue.

At first the doctrine of closely regulated industries was limited to businesses with a long history of pervasive regulation, such as liquor and firearms, but the list has expanded over the years as the Supreme Court has deferred to the legislature's judgment about what industries are, in fact, closely regulated. One court was so deferential that it found barbering to be a closely regulated industry! With such precedents on the books, Fourth Amendment scholar John Wesley Hall Jr. warns, "The government can now impose the warrant exception on practically any industry which it could conceivably regulate."[40]

The EPA's License to Trespass

A number of federal environmental laws explicitly authorize warrantless inspections of commercial premises. Section 6927(a) of RCRA, for example, provides,

> For purposes of developing or assisting in the development
> of any regulation or enforcing the provisions of this chapter,
> such officers, employees or representatives are authorized—
> (1) to enter at reasonable times any establishment or other
> place where hazardous wastes are or have been generated,
> stored, treated, disposed of, or transported from;
> (2) to inspect and obtain samples from any person of any
> such wastes and samples of any containers or labeling for
> such wastes.

RCRA makes it a crime for a company to refuse entry to EPA investigators.[41] Such statutes can withstand constitutional challenge because of the closely regulated industry doctrine.[42] Agriculture, food sales, commercial fishing, and hazardous waste disposal have already been designated by the courts as closely regulated industries for purposes of Fourth Amendment analysis. In light of the plethora of environmental rules concerning air, water, and "ecosystems," the alarming question for civil libertarians and businesspeople is which industries will *not* fall into the closely regulated exception to the administrative warrant requirement. In 1987 Justice William Brennan recognized that the so-called exception was well on its way to becoming the rule: "If New York City's administrative scheme renders the vehicle-dismantling business closely regulated, few businesses will escape such a finding."[43]

Although the closely regulated industry doctrine poses the most serious threat to Fourth Amendment privacy rights, there are at least three other significant search-and-seizure problems:

First, the lower probable cause standard for the issuance of administrative warrants has spawned interagency "bootstrapping" searches. One of the original justifications for the administrative warrant was the notion that the government was interested only in making sure that civil regulations were being followed. In *Camara v. United States* (1967), for example, the Supreme Court noted, "A routine inspection of the physical condition of private property [was] a less hostile intrusion than a typical policeman's search for the fruits and instrumentalities of crime."[44] With that distinction in mind, the Court held that administrative warrants did not have to meet the probable cause standard that had been set for criminal matters.

The criminalization of environmental infractions, however, means that the courts must now grapple with situations in which prosecutors and investigators have used administrative inspections as pretexts for searching for evidence of criminal activity. The Environmental Crimes Unit of the Federal Bureau of Investigation, for example, has enlisted the help of local health officials in gathering evidence for criminal prosecutions when the local officials conduct their "routine" inspections.[45] The Supreme Court appears to be untroubled by such interagency cooperation. A 1987 decision held that "the discovery of evidence of crimes in the course of an otherwise proper administrative inspection does not render that search illegal or the administrative scheme suspect."[46]

Second, ranchers and farmers have no Fourth Amendment protection from governmental agents who want to trespass on "open fields." In *Oliver v. United States* (1984), the Supreme Court held that a governmental "intrusion upon . . . open fields is not [an] unreasonable search proscribed by the text of the Fourth Amendment."[47] The *Oliver* ruling effectively gives federal and state agents carte blanche to trespass on private land to conduct searches and to monitor private activity. Agents of the U.S. Fish and Wildlife Service, for example, trespassed on a Maryland farm without a warrant when they suspected a possible violation of the Migratory Bird Treaty Act. The agents discovered that Paul Swann had failed to remove a strip of corn from his land before the first day of hunting season, which is apparently what the law decreed. Swann was prosecuted for "aiding and abetting the taking or attempted taking of migratory waterfowl with the aid of bait."[48]

Third, government agencies do not have to obtain a warrant to inspect garbage bags from apartment houses and homes. In 1988 many conservative lawyers and commentators scoffed when civil libertarians urged the Supreme Court to overturn a drug conviction that was secured through a warrantless police search of garbage bags. With more and more communities enacting mandatory recycling statutes, those conservatives may rue the day the Supreme Court sanctioned such searches. In New York City, for example, "recycling cops" rummage through neighborhood garbage during the early morning hours and impose fines on individuals and businesses for "noncompliance."[49] If history is any guide, the penalties for recycling violations will get stiffer in the years to come as environmental groups pressure lawmakers to "get tough" with repeat offenders.

The warrant and probable-cause safeguards of the Fourth Amendment have suffered serious erosion in recent years. Lawmakers and prosecutors who are sympathetic to the environmental agenda have taken advantage of the Supreme Court's dubious precedents to extend the regulatory hand of government. The abuses that have followed will not cease until the courts return to first principles. Ideally, of course, the judiciary should apply the traditional probable-cause criteria to all governmental inspections of private property.[50] The "administrative" search warrant, which was created out of whole cloth by the judiciary, should be jettisoned.

Such a far-reaching and principled reform, however, is not likely to occur in the short term. It is therefore appropriate to consider a few interim measures that would help to curb the most egregious bureaucratic overreaching. First, the wide-open doctrine of "closely regulated" industries ought to be brought within the procedural framework of administrative warrants. Second, lawmakers ought to require administrative agencies to obtain inspection warrants in nonemergency situations.[51] If the Fourth Amendment means anything, it means that the propriety of a search cannot rest on the unreviewable discretion of law enforcement officials and administrative bureaucrats. In nonemergency situations, those officials should have to obtain a warrant from an independent magistrate. To paraphrase Judge Prettyman, environmental laws ought to be subject to the same constitutional limitations as other police powers.[52] If those modest steps are not taken soon, the Fourth Amendment will lose all vitality.

Liability without Fault

One of the principal differences between an ordinary criminal prosecution and an environmental prosecution concerns the issue of criminal intent. In ordinary criminal prosecutions, the government has to prove that the accused had some prescribed bad state of mind. That principle was expressed by the Latin maxim *actus not facit reum nisi mens sit rea* (an act does not make one guilty unless his mind is guilty).[53]

The Question of Intent

By the same token, bad thoughts alone do not constitute a crime if there is no "bad act." If a policeman discovers a diary that someone has accidently dropped on the sidewalk, and the contents include references to wanting to steal the possessions of another, the author cannot be prosecuted for a crime. The basic idea, of course, is that the government should not be in the business of punishing "bad thoughts."

When *mens rea* (evil intent) and *actus reus* (evil act) were fundamental prerequisites for criminal activity, no person could be branded a "criminal" until a prosecutor could persuade a jury that the accused possessed "an evil-meaning mind with an evil-doing hand."[54] That understanding of crime—as a compound concept—was firmly entrenched in the English common law at the time of the American Revolution.

Punishment without Intent or Action

Although the common law requirements of *mens rea* and *actus reus* are still considered necessary for ordinary criminal convictions—such as assault and burglary—many of the major federal environmental laws dispense with one or both of those elements. The Refuse Act, for example, dispenses with *mens rea* so that criminal intent is irrelevant to guilt. In 1974 the White Fuel Corporation was prosecuted under the Refuse Act when the Coast Guard discovered that oil from a storage tank on the company's shoreline property was seeping into Boston Harbor. The trial court "denied White Fuel's offer to present evidence that it had not known of the underground deposit, had not appreciated its hazards, and had acted diligently when the deposit became known."[55] The trial judge found that, under the Refuse Act, the seepage was a "public welfare offense" and that the government did not have to prove any malevolent purpose or even negligence.

The Clean Air Act and Comprehensive Environmental Response, Compensation and Liability Act (CERCLA) also dispense with *mens rea*. In 1991 Paul Buckley was prosecuted under those statutes when some asbestos was released into the environment in the course of a demolition project. No one was injured, but regulations were violated. The trial court told the jury that the government did not have "to prove a wrongful intent or awareness of wrongdoing." The question of whether Buckley acted in good faith was deemed "immaterial" to the case. On appeal, Buckley's attorneys argued that those instructions "violated due process by eliminating knowledge as an element of the crimes."[56] The appellate court affirmed Buckley's conviction because "the very nature of asbestos" and other hazardous substances put those who deal with them "on notice that they may incur criminal liability for emission-related actions."

Hunters and farmers are routinely ensnared by the Migratory Bird Treaty Act (MBTA) for inadvertent violations. In 1989 prosecutors brought criminal charges against Ronald Rollins, an Idaho farmer. Rollins applied a mixture of registered pesticides to 50 acres of seed alfalfa growing on his farm. A flock of geese came to the field, ate the alfalfa, and died from ingesting the pesticides. The magistrate found Rollins guilty even though he had applied the chemicals "in the recommended quantities [and] at the appropriate time."[57] The fact that the farming community had used the pesticides "for a number of years without major incident" was irrelevant because the MBTA imposes strict liability on anyone who kills a migratory bird.

It is difficult to see what purpose is served by such heavy-handed enforcement. Those "environmental criminals" did not deserve to be hauled into court like common thieves. They did not set out to break the law, nor were they cutting corners in an attempt to increase their profit margins. The argument that such prosecutions will deter others is without merit. As Henry M. Hart Jr. notes in *Law and Contemporary Problems*, there is an "inherent unlikelihood that people's behavior will be significantly affected by commands that are not definitely brought to their attention."[58] But even if a string of prosecutions prompted every Midwestern farmer to memorize the provisions of the MBTA, how in the world could farmers possibly keep the birds off their crops?

Federal environmental laws have also dispensed with the *actus reus* requirement. In 1982 Congress expanded the legal definition of "person" in the Clean Air Act and the Clean Water Act to include "any responsible corporate officer."[59] Those amendments will allow prosecutors to indict corporate chief executive officers for the acts and omissions of low-level employees.[60] Once the government has shown that a company employee has run afoul of a regulation, the prosecutor merely has to get hold of the corporate organizational chart to indict executives.[61] The *mens rea* of corporate officers can usually be established by inference from circumstantial evidence. As one legal treatise explains, "Environmental laws permit the presumption of [guilty] knowledge under a myriad of circumstances."[62] The courts, for example, allow juries to draw inferences about a corporate officer's knowledge from evidence indicating a "hands-on management style."[63] The courts also allow juries to infer criminal intent from "circumstantial evidence of lax management practices."[64]

Over the past 70 years lawmakers have so lowered the standards for criminal liability that the traditional distinctions between civil liability and criminal liability are vanishing.[65] As a result, indictment and conviction under America's environmental criminal laws are rapidly losing any associated stigma because the general public does not accept all of the government's environmental norms as legitimate and deserving of compliance. There may indeed be a place for criminal sanctions in environmental regulation, but the threshold for such sanctions should be very high. Reform of current law should begin with the immediate reintroduction of the *mens rea* and *actus reus* requirements to environmental criminal law.

Double Prosecutions and Double Jeopardy

The Fifth Amendment's double jeopardy clause bars government from subjecting any person to multiple prosecutions for the same offense. But that provision has been interpreted in a way that allows separate state and federal prosecutions for the same conduct. That "dual sovereignty" exception places enormous power in the hands of those prosecuting environmental crimes.

The Creeping Power of "Dual Prosecution"

Outside of the drug war context, there may be no other area of the law with as much potential for dual prosecution abuse as environmental criminal law. Many states have enacted environmental regulations that mirror the major federal environmental statutes. The very existence of such overlapping statutes creates a danger of arbitrary multiple prosecutions. The danger is heightened when state and federal officials work together on investigative task forces, and when the money generated from criminal and civil fines is plowed back into the budgets of the various enforcement agencies.

When defendants in environmental cases invoke the double jeopardy principle in successive prosecutions, the courts invariably reject the argument on the basis of the Supreme Court's "dual sovereignty" doctrine. In *United States v. Louisville Edible Products Inc.* (1991), for example, the federal government brought charges against a Kentucky corporation under the Clean Air Act.[66] Since the federal charges were based on conduct for which the company had already been fined by a local environmental enforcement agency, the company argued that it was protected by the Double Jeopardy clause of the Fifth Amendment. The federal appellate court found that claim to be "misplaced." Following Supreme Court precedents, the court simply noted that the case involved successive prosecutions by separate sovereigns and that each sovereign could "pursue claims against Louisville Edible for the same conduct without subjecting the defendant to double jeopardy."[67] An EPA Enforcement Accomplishments Report lauded the decision for its important "precedential" value.[68]

The dual sovereignty exception to the double jeopardy principle is based on the notions that each sovereign has different interests and that those interests can be advanced only by multiple prosecutions. That rationale is infirm. Even if that rationale was an accurate description of our federalist legal system 100 years ago, it is obviously at odds with modern practices. As Daniel A. Braun observes in the *American Journal of Criminal Law*, "In light of the extensive cooperation between state and federal law enforcement officials, the story of two independent sovereigns pursuing their independent goals is a transparent fiction."[69] That is especially true in the environmental context. First, the major federal environmental statutes invite the states to participate in the federal regulatory program. The Clean Water Act, for example, explicitly contemplates "a partnership between the States and the Federal government."[70] And the courts readily acknowledge that such partnerships are "animated by a shared objective."[71]

Second, the federal regulatory structure has created a situation in which state and federal officials have frequent and regular contact with one another. In testimony before Congress in 1989, then deputy assistant attorney general George W. Van Cleve boasted about the close contact his office had enjoyed with environmental investigators and prosecutors on the state level: "We regard the process of criminal enforcement of environmental law as very much a cooperative process. On a daily basis we work with our colleagues from the States and rely on them for much of our information, resources, and prosecutorial assistance."[72]

There is, of course, nothing inherently wrong with cooperation between federal and state officials. The issue is whether those officials ought to be able to "harass the accused so as to deny him his protection under the Fifth Amendment."[73] After all, if a Justice

Department official can pick up a telephone and have a state prosecutor initiate criminal proceedings against a person who has just been acquitted of charges in federal court, the double jeopardy clause might as well not exist.

Environmentalists point out that there have been only a few reported cases of dual prosecution. Although that is technically true, it gives a distorted impression of how the criminal law is actually administered. No one would dispute the proposition that the dual sovereignty doctrine gives the prosecution enormous leverage over defendants in plea negotiations. Since approximately 95 percent of the cases in America's criminal justice system never go to trial, any abuse will become readily apparent in plea bargaining. If an industrial accident occurs at an oil refinery operated by a midsized company, for example, and federal prosecutors bring criminal charges under environmental law, the chief executive officer must face the reality of the government's dual prosecution powers. Even if the CEO sincerely believes that no criminal law was violated, he cannot ignore his fiduciary responsibility to weigh the costs of a legal battle. The decision is a tough one. Even if a jury acquits the company in federal court, another prosecution may be initiated in state court. And even if a second jury acquits, prosecutors can pursue stiff civil fines in both state and federal court. Because of the costs of attorneys' fees and the adverse publicity that would accompany a drawn-out fight, medium- and small-sized businesses will probably decide to "cut their losses" and plead guilty to the lowest criminal charge and pay the lowest fine that their attorneys can negotiate. In such a climate, only large corporations and individuals who have the financial wherewithal to wage a battle have a chance of successfully resisting flimsy and unsubstantiated charges.[74] If the double jeopardy principle were respected and only one criminal trial were possible, more defendants would be able to force prosecutors to prove their allegations in a court of law.

It is interesting that the Supreme Court will not tolerate dual prosecutions when the separate sovereigns are city and state governments.[75] In such situations, the Court allows city and state agencies to work together to bring the strongest possible case against a lawbreaker—but only one prosecution is permitted for any given act. That simple rule ought to apply with equal force when the sovereigns happen to be the federal and state governments.

"Self-Confession" Programs and Self-Incrimination

In the environmental crimes context, federal and state governments have successfully perverted the Fifth Amendment privilege against self-incrimination. Environmental law seems to be the only area of the law where it could be a crime not to report a crime. The "compliance data" that the EPA and state authorities monitor are derived "almost entirely from self-reporting requirements."[76] As unbelievable as it may seem, environmental "criminals," unlike burglars and rapists, are expected to reveal their identities whenever a rule or regulation is violated.[77] Should a corporate executive or the manager of a small business fail to confess regulatory violations in a timely manner, prosecutors promise crippling, no-holds-barred enforcement actions.[78]

Government Power Begins to "Evolve"

Elaborate environmental regulatory systems have been constructed at both the state and federal levels, and those systems are replete with reporting and recordkeeping requirements. As one environmental law treatise notes, "[T]he new [sentencing] guidelines place companies between the Scylla of reporting an offense that might otherwise go undetected by the government and the Charybdis of a finding of nondisclosure, noncooperation, or, still worse, active concealment."[79]

Ordinary criminal suspects enjoy the constitutional option of remaining silent during an official inquiry, but environmental criminal suspects have no choice but to cooperate with regulators as they proceed with their inspections and investigations. The Toxic Substances Control Act, for example, gives the EPA the authority to subpoena any report, paper, or document that the agency "deems necessary."[80] The EPA can even subpoena "answers to questions."[81] Such prosecutorial powers are unheard of outside of the regulatory context. According to the modern constitutional orthodoxy, agents of the FBI have an affirmative obligation to warn suspected bank robbers and kidnappers about the consequences of uttering an incriminating statement, but EPA investigators have been given the constitutional power to coerce confessions of environmental infractions from businesspeople.

The penalties for noncompliance with reporting requirements are serious—and so are prosecutors. A Missouri corporation, for example, was indicted because it failed to report an oil spill in the Mississippi River. In that case, a low-level employee was the only witness, and he kept the information to himself. Despite the fact that no officer or director of the corporation was aware of the spill, the company was prosecuted. A $20,000 fine was upheld on appeal because of a legal fiction that says, "The knowledge of the employees is the knowledge of the corporation."[82]

The federal reporting regulations have remarkable breadth. A "reportable release" under CERCLA, for example, includes

> any spilling, leaking, pumping, pouring, emitting, emptying, discharging, injecting, escaping, leaching, dumping, or disposing into the environment (including the abandonment or discarding of barrels, containers, and other closed receptacles containing any hazardous substance or pollutant or contaminant). . . .[83]

The definitions are so comprehensive that innocuous activities can trigger legal obligations under federal criminal law. A New York maintenance supervisor, for example, was criminally prosecuted under CERCLA because he had a work crew bury old cans of waste paint. When the supervisor steadfastly refused to plead guilty to a criminal offense, the Justice Department filed a 43-count indictment against him. The jury rejected all of the charges except two: the notification counts. The defendant, David Carr, now has a criminal record because he failed to notify federal authorities of the burial of old cans of paint.[84]

Environmentalists extol the noble purpose of the reporting regulations. They point out that two public policy objectives are advanced by notification requirements. First, such regulations provide government officials with pertinent information about the scope of industrial accidents and the risks associated with possible fallout. Innocent lives might be saved by public dissemination of information about such accidents. Second, a timely report would prompt initiation of a government-supervised cleanup effort, which would probably lessen the risk of any additional damage to the environment.

The legitimacy of those government objectives cannot be denied, nor are environmental notification procedures unconstitutional per se. The Fifth Amendment only prevents the government from prosecuting an individual or company for something it reports. The public policy objectives of the notification requirements are not lost when prosecutorial immunity attaches. And prosecutorial immunity does not mean polluters will escape the consequences of their actions.

The government would still be able to pursue an irresponsible polluter for cleanup costs under civil law. Private individuals and corporations who are harmed by pollution would also be able to sue polluters for proven damages. There is, in short, no conflict between the privilege against self-incrimination and workable environmental policies.

Conclusion

In its zeal to stamp out pollution, the federal government has assumed extraordinary police and prosecutorial powers over the citizenry. Instead of developing environmental policies within the American constitutional framework, federal and state actors have relentlessly sought the modification of constitutional principles to accommodate their own regulatory agendas.[85] That growing threat to civil liberties is frightfully real. The idea that Americans must sacrifice their constitutional rights to "save the earth" has been gaining currency in the legislative chamber and in the courtroom for 25 years. To reverse that dangerous trend, Congress should take the following actions:

- Reduce the injustice of vaguely written environmental rules by restoring traditional legal defenses such as diligence, good faith, and actual knowledge.[86]
- Restore the rule of lenity for environmental criminal cases by enacting a statute that will explicitly provide for the "strict construction" of federal criminal laws.[87]
- Limit prosecutorial discretion with respect to the decision to charge. Most regulatory violations should be handled through civil enforcement procedures. Criminal enforcement should be reserved for flagrant or repetitive violations of law. Congress should either legislatively mandate that administrative or civil remedies are prerequisite to criminal proceedings or require U.S. attorneys to seek authorization from the attorney general before filing criminal charges in environmental cases.[88]
- Restore Fourth Amendment privacy rights by repealing every federal law that authorizes warrantless entry onto private property. Absent consent or exigent circumstances, government agents should be required to obtain a warrant from an independent magistrate.

- Restore the traditional elements of criminal liability—*mens rea* and *actus reus*—to environmental law. Congress should abolish the doctrine of strict criminal liability as well as the "responsible corporate officer" doctrine. Those theories of criminal liability are completely inconsistent with the Anglo-American tradition and have no place in a free society.
- Restore the Fifth Amendment guarantee against double jeopardy by flatly prohibiting successive prosecutions by federal and state agencies. As an alternative, Congress could require U.S. attorneys to seek authorization from the attorney general before initiating a successive prosecution.
- Restore the Fifth Amendment privilege against self-incrimination by extending prosecutorial immunity to reporting and recordkeeping requirements. The abominable practice of compulsory self-incrimination should cease immediately.

Those reform measures should be only the beginning of a fundamental reexamination of the role of the federal government, as well as the role of the criminal sanction, in environmental law. If more significant reforms are not forthcoming, federal and state agencies will continue to run roughshod over constitutional principles. In the present climate it is especially important for Americans to understand that the Bill of Rights is incapable of enforcing itself. That task necessarily falls upon the organizations and citizens who wish to retain their rights. Private individuals and organizations must exert pressure on legislators and judges through litigation, public criticism, and elections. If the American people continue to allow their legislators and judges to rationalize exceptions to time-honored principles, the Bill of Rights will eventually be emptied of all content, and that would be the greatest crime of all.

This is an abridged version of a study originally published as Cato Institute Policy Analysis no. 223, April 20, 1995.

Notes

1. "The Constitution is the rock of our political salvation; it is the palladium of our rights; . . . [but] when the [government] pursues a favorite object with passionate enthusiasm, men are too apt, in their eager embrace of it, to overlook the means by which it is attained. These are the melancholy occasions when the barriers of the government are broken down and the boundaries of the Constitution defaced." Junius Americanus [pseud.], letter, *New York Daily Advertiser*, July 13, 1790; quoted in Charles

Warren, *Congress, The Constitution, and The Supreme Court* (Boston: Little, Brown, 1930), p. 105.

2. See, for example, "Justice Department Announces Record $2 Billion Year for Environmental Enforcement," *U.S. Newswire* press release, October 29, 1992; and "Justice Department Announces Third Straight Record Year for Environmental Enforcement," *U.S. Newswire* press release, May 8, 1992.

3. See Celia Campbell-Mohn, Barry Breen, and J. William Futrell, *Sustainable Environmental Law* (St. Paul: West, 1993), p. 13. The authors note that "Congress [eventually] used creeping federalization rather than direct legislation because it [remained] unclear whether the federal government could constitutionally operate air and water pollution programs" (p. 38). For a persuasive case that the federal government is not authorized to operate comprehensive air and water pollution programs, see Roger Pilon, "A Government of Limited Powers," *The Cato Handbook for Congress* (Washington: Cato Institute, 1995), pp. 17–35.

4. 33 U.S.C. 407.

5. Campbell-Mohn, Breen, and Futrell, p. 55. See also F. Henry Habicht II, "The Federal Perspective on Environmental Criminal Enforcement: How to Remain on the Civil Side," *Environmental Law Reporter* 17 (1987): 10479.

6. Nan Robertson, "Earth's Day, Like Mother's, Pulls Capital Together," *New York Times*, April 23, 1970, p. 30.

7. On Nelson, see "Earth Day: Five Who Care," *Look*, April 21, 1970, p. 33. Humphrey was quoted in Gladwin Hill, "Activity Ranges from Oratory to Legislation," *New York Times*, April 23, 1970, p. 1.

8. See Paul R. Portney, ed., *Public Policies for Environmental Protection* (Washington: Resources for the Future, 1990), p. 10. See also Budget of the United States Government, Fiscal Year 1996: Historical Tables, Table 4.1, pp. 59, 62; and Budget of the United States Government, Fiscal Year 1996: Analytical Perspectives, Table 12-1, p. 180. Even adjusting for inflation, the EPA budget has more than doubled from $2.6 billion to more than $6 billion.

9. See Richard Thornburgh, "Criminal Enforcement of Environmental Laws—A National Priority," *George Washington Law Review* 59 (1991): 776 n. 3.

10. See Joseph G. Block, "Environmental Criminal Enforcement in the 1990s," *Villanova Environmental Law Journal* 3 (1992): 37.

11. Personal communication of the author with Brett Grosko of the Policy, Legislation and Special Litigation Section of the Environment and Natural Resources Division, U.S. Department of Justice, March 24, 1995; and Henry J. Reske, "Record EPA Prosecutions," *ABA Journal*, March 1992, p. 25.

12. Christopher Harris, Raymond C. Marshall, and Patrick O. Cavanaugh, *Environmental Crimes* (Colorado Springs: Shepard's/McGraw-Hill, 1994), p. INT-8. See also Kenneth A. Grady and Craig H. Zimmerman, "Preparing for the Onslaught: Search Warrants and Inspections in Environmental Criminal Cases," *Natural Resources & Environment* 8 (1994): 7. "It is impossible to be in 100 percent compliance with all the environmental laws all the time, and a candid EPA manager will admit as much" (p. 54).

13. Quoted in Jonathan Weber, "Corporate Crime of the '90s," *Los Angeles Times*, November 25, 1989, p. A1.

14. Nadine Strossen, as president of the American Civil Liberties Union, has observed, "The central principle of the Bill of Rights is the indivisibility of rights. If any person or any group is deprived of any right, then all rights are endangered

for all people and all groups." Strossen, "Politically Correct Speech and the First Amendment," *Cato Policy Report* 13, no. 2 (March-April 1991): 6. Many environmental activists appreciate that point. Eco-activist Nancy Burnet, for example, has noted the importance of standing up for other people's rights. "You'd better do it, because your rights could be at stake next," she said. Quoted in Rik Scarce, *Eco-Warriors: Understanding the Radical Environmental Movement* (Chicago: Noble, 1990), p. 264.

15. *Connally v. General Const. Co.*, 269 U.S. 385, 391 (1926).

16. At least one lawyer has been indicted for advising a client to not clean up waste. Don J. DeBenedictis, "Hazardous Advice," *ABA Journal*, September 1991, p. 16.

17. See *Parker v. Levy*, 417 U.S. 773 (1973) (Stewart, J., dissenting). "The absence of specificity in a criminal statute invites abuse on the part of prosecuting officials, who are left free to harass any individuals or groups who may be the object of official displeasure" (p. 775).

18. *United States v. Wiltberger*, 18 U.S. 76, 96 (1820). "The rule that penal laws are to be construed strictly, is perhaps not much less old than [judicial] construction itself" (p. 95). See also *United States v. Bass*, 404 U.S. 336, 347–48 (1971); and *Liparota v. United States*, 471 U.S. 419, 427 (1985).

19. *Papachristou v. City of Jacksonville*, 405 U.S. 156, 162 (1972); and *Boyce Motor Lines v. United States*, 342 U.S. 337, 340 (1952).

20. "[It is] not unfair to require that one who deliberately goes perilously close to an area of proscribed conduct shall take the risk that he may cross the line." Ibid. Compare *Ricks v. District of Columbia*, 414 F.2d 1097 (1968). "Liberty under law extends to the full range of conduct which the individual is free to pursue. Since most people shy away from legal violations, personal liberty is unconstitutionally dampened when one can but doubt whether he is actually free to pursue particular conduct" (p. 1101).

21. Marianne Lavelle, "Environmental Vise: Law, Compliance," *National Law Journal*, August 30, 1993, p. S8.

22. See *American Min. Congress v. U.S. E.P.A.*, 824 F.2d 1177, 1189 (1987).

23. 384 U.S. 224, 226 (1966).

24. Ibid., p. 234 (Harlan, Black, and Stewart, J.J., dissenting). Notwithstanding the strong argument of the dissenters, federal courts often rely on the Standard Oil precedent for the proposition that "federal water pollution laws, including their penal provisions, are [to be] construed in a broad, rather than a narrow fashion." See *United States v. Boldt*, 929 F.2d 35, 41 (1991). See also Paul G. Nittoly, "Environmental Criminal Cases: The Dawn of a New Era," *Seton Hall Law Review* 21 (1991): 1135–36.

25. 391 F. Supp. 1181 (1975).

26. Ibid., p. 1187 Emphasis added.

27. Former attorney general Richard Thornburgh acknowledged that the felony charges brought against the Exxon Corporation for the 1990 oil spill in Alaska's Prince William Sound were based on an "innovative" legal theory. See Mary Ellen Kris and Gail L. Vannelli, "Today's Criminal Environmental Enforcement Program: Why You May Be Vulnerable and Why You Should Guard against Prosecution through an Environmental Audit," *Columbia Journal of Environmental Law* 16 (1991): 237.

28. This is another important difference between ordinary street criminals and environmental "criminals." Attorney Paul Kamenar writes, "Bank robbers and rapists cannot be hauled before an Administrative Law Judge or civilly enjoined; the only remedy society has chosen for these *malum in se* crimes is criminal punishment."

Kamenar, "The Truth: 'There Are No Environmental Crimes,' " *California Lawyer*, August 1993, p. 89.

29. Quoted in Leslie Spencer, "Designated Inmates," *Forbes*, October 26, 1992, p. 100. See also Kevin A. Gaynor, Jodi C. Remer, and Thomas R. Bartman, "Environmental Criminal Prosecutions: Simple Fixes for a Flawed System," *Villanova Environmental Law Journal* 3 (1992): 1–31. "[W]hether a violation is treated criminally, civilly or administratively is more a function of what type of investigator learns of the violation first and in what judicial district the violation occurs, not the nature or environmental severity of the violation" (p. 4).

30. James Madison, *Federalist Paper* 62, in *The Federalist Papers*, ed. Clinton Rossiter (New York: New American Library, 1961), p. 381.

31. William L. Gardner and Adam H. Steinman, " 'Knowing' Remains Key Word," *National Law Journal*, September 2, 1991, p. 28. See also *Heckler v. Community Health Services of Crawford County, Inc.*, 467 U.S. 51 (1984). "[T]hose who deal with the Government are expected to know the law and may not rely on the conduct of government agents to the contrary" (p. 63). Campbell-Mohn, Breen, and Futrell point out that "[t]rying to 'know' environmental law may be impossible. There is too much of it" (p. 66).

32. Quoted in William P. Kucewicz, "Grime and Punishment," *ECO*, June 1993, p. 54.

33. Steven J. Wax, "The Fourth Amendment, Administrative Searches and the Loss of Liberty," *Environmental Law* 18 (1988): 912.

34. *District of Columbia v. Little*, 178 F.2d 13, 17 (1949).

35. *Camara v. Municipal Court*, 387 U.S. 523, 528–29 (1967).

36. 328 U.S. 582 (1946).

37. 452 U.S. 594, 598 (1981).

38. Quoted in John Wesley Hall Jr., *Search and Seizure*, 2d ed. (New York: Clark Boardman Callaghan, 1991) vol. 2, p. 376.

39. 406 U.S. 311 (1972).

40. Hall, vol. 2, p. 390.

41. 42 U.S.C. 6928(d). See also Harris, Marshall, and Cavanaugh, pp. 2–17, in which the authors note that it is a felony under the Clean Air Act for a company to refuse an inspection of an "emissions source"; and Eva M. Fromm, "Commanding Respect: Criminal Sanctions for Environmental Crimes," *St. Mary's Law Journal* 21 (1990): 839–40, in which she discusses sanctions under the Toxic Substances Control Act.

42. See *National Standard Co. v. Adamkus*, 685 F. Supp. 1040, 1046 n. 5 (1988); and *Commonwealth of Pennsylvania v. Fiore*, 526 A.2d 704 (1986).

43. *New York v. Burger*, 482 U.S. 691, 721 (1987) (Brennan, J., dissenting).

44. 387 U.S. 523, 530 (1967).

45. See Spencer, p. 100. See also the discussion of cooperation between the Occupational Safety and Health Administration and the EPA in James M. Strock, "Environmental Criminal Enforcement Priorities for the 1990s," *George Washington Law Review* 59 (1991): 925 n. 48.

46. *New York v. Burger*, 482 U.S. 691, 716 (1987).

47. *Oliver v. United States*, 466 U.S. 170, 177 (1984). See also Robert W. Martin Jr., "EPA and Administrative Inspections," *Florida State University Law Review* 7 (1979): 123–37.

48. *United States v. Swann*, 377 F. Supp. 1305 (1974). See also *Dow Chemical Co. v. United States*, 476 U.S. 227 (1986); *Air Pollution Variance Board v. Western Alfalfa*, 416 U.S. 861 (1974); and *Department of Environmental Protection v. Emerson*, 616 A.2d 1268, 1271 (1992).

49. See Allan R. Gold, "For 'Recycling Cops,' Dragnets Turn Up Bottles," *New York Times*, November 23, 1990, p. B1. The Supreme Court sanctioned the warrantless search and seizure of garbage left for collection in *California v. Greenwood*, 486 U.S. 35 (1988).

50. For some historical evidence that this is the appropriate rule, see Dennis Stewart, "Administrative Searches and the Fourth Amendment: The Definition of 'Probable Cause' in *Camara v. Municipal Court of the City and County of San Francisco*," *University of Missouri-Kansas City Law Review* 36 (1968): 127 n. 85.

51. "[T]he most logical constitutional approach would be to require administrative inspection warrants in all situations where voluntary informed consent is not given, or where 'emergency circumstances' . . . do not exist." Michael R. Sonnenreich and Robert G. Pinco, "The Inspector Knocks: Administrative Inspection Warrants under an Expanded Fourth Amendment," *Southwestern Law Journal* 24 (1970): 434.

52. See Little, p. 20. See also *Frank v. Maryland*, 359 U.S. 360, 382 (1959) (Douglas, J., dissenting).

53. Wayne R. LaFave and Austin W. Scott Jr., *Criminal Law*, 2d ed. (St. Paul: West, 1986), p. 212.

54. Quoted in *Morissette v. United States*, 342 U.S. 251 (1952).

55. *United States v. White Fuel Corporation*, 498 F.2d 619, 621 (1974).

56. *United States v. Buckley*, 934 F.2d 84, 87 (1991).

57. *United States v. Rollins*, 706 F. Supp. 742, 743 (1989). Although it is true that Rollins's conviction was overturned by a sympathetic federal district court, the case is yet another example of the injustices that take place when legislators pass strict liability legislation and then rely on the "sound discretion" of prosecutors with respect to case selection. Rollins is entitled to a full pardon and ought to be fully compensated for any legal expenses he incurred.

58. Henry M. Hart Jr., "The Aims of the Criminal Law," *Law and Contemporary Problems* 23 (1958): 431.

59. Clean Air Act, 42 U.S.C. 7413(c)(3) (1982); and Clean Water Act, 33 U.S.C. 1319(c)(3) (1982).

60. "[T]he willfulness or negligence of the actor [will] be imputed to him by virtue of his position of responsibility." *United States v. Brittain*, 931 F.2d 1413, 1419 (1991). See also *United States v. Johnson & Towers, Inc.*, 741 F.2d 662, 665 n. 3 (1984).

61. "Often, the responsible corporate officer will have played no role in the offense other than having failed to prevent it." Lisa Ann Harig, "Ignorance Is Not Bliss: Responsible Corporate Officers Convicted of Environmental Crimes and the Federal Sentencing Guidelines," *Duke Law Journal* 42 (1992): 162.

62. Harris, Marshall, and Cavanaugh, pp. 5–11.

63. See *United States v. MacDonald & Watson Waste Oil Co.*, 933 F.2d 35, 50 (1991).

64. Harris, Marshall, and Cavanaugh, pp. 5–11.

65. See Benjamin S. Sharp, "Environmental Enforcement Excesses: Overcriminalization and Too Severe Punishment," *Environmental Law Reporter* 21 (1991): 10658. See also James V. DeLong, "The Criminalization of Just About Everything," *American Enterprise*, March-April 1994, p. 26; and John C. Coffee Jr., "Does 'Unlawful' Mean

'Criminal'?: Reflections on the Disappearing Tort/Crime Distinction in American Law," *Boston University Law Review* 71 (1991): 193.

66. 926 F.2d 584 (1991).

67. Ibid., p. 587.

68. *EPA, Enforcement Accomplishments Report: FY 1993*, pp. 3–85.

69. Braun, p. 10.

70. See *Arkansas v. Oklahoma*, 60 U.S.L.W. 4176, 4178 (1992).

71. Ibid. See also *United States v. Colorado*, 990 F.2d 1565 (1993).

72. U.S. House Committee on the Judiciary, Environmental Crimes Act: Hearing on H.R. 3641 before the Subcommittee on Criminal Justice of the House Committee on the Judiciary, 101st Cong., 1st sess., December 12, 1989, p. 41. Robert Abrams, attorney general of New York, has said, "Looking to the future, it is certain that state and federal authorities will increasingly cooperate in their prosecutions." Abrams, "The Maturing Discipline of Environmental Prosecution," *Columbia Journal of Environmental Law* 16 (1991): 279.

73. Bartkus, p. 169 (Brennan, J., dissenting).

74. Thus, "in the Valdez oil spill case, a top Justice Department attorney began to signal—after a proposed $500 million settlement with Exxon collapsed—that the federal government might not be able to support the long-reaching, novel indictment it had brought under little-used environmental laws." Stanley S. Arkin, "Be a Good Corporate Citizen: Fight the Feds," *Wall Street Journal*, March 13, 1990.

75. See *Waller v. Florida*, 397 U.S. 387 (1970).

76. Robert W. Adler and Charles Lord, "Environmental Crimes: Raising the Stakes," *George Washington Law Review* 59 (1991): 813. See also Paul R. Portney, ed., *Public Policies for Environmental Protection* (Washington: Resources for the Future, 1990), pp. 249–53; and Lee Fisher, "Environmental Compliance," *Daily Register*, March 18, 1994, p. 3.

77. The Toxic Substances Control Act (TSCA), for example, requires the owner of any polychlorinated biphenyl (PCB) equipment to report any spill of 10 or more pounds of material containing PCBs at concentrations of 50 ppm or greater. See 40 CFR 761.120-.135. This regulatory system has been aptly referred to as the "TSCA self-confession program." EPA, *Enforcement in the 1990s Project: Recommendations of the Analytical Workgroups* (October, 1991), p. 5-1.

78. "Companies will have the book thrown at them . . . if it is determined that managers have condoned or concealed crimes." Linda Himelstein and Catherine Yang, "A Warning Shot to Scare Polluters Straight," *Business Week*, November 22, 1993, p. 60. The federal sentencing guidelines "place an unprecedented premium on self-disclosure." Harris, Marshall, and Cavanaugh, pp. 9–20.

79. Harris, Marshall, and Cavanaugh, pp. 9–20.

80. 15 U.S.C. 2610(c).

81. Ibid.

82. *Apex Oil Co. v. United States*, 530 F.2d 1291, 1295 (1976). See also *United States v. Texas Pipe Line Co.*, 528 F. Supp. 728, 733 (1978), in which reporting requirements of the Clean Water Act are held not to violate the privilege against self-incrimination.

83. 42 U.S.C. 9601(22).

84. *United States v. Carr*, 880 F.2d 1550 (1989).

85. For an environmental vision that is consistent with the American constitutional framework, see Jerry Taylor, "Environmental Reform," in *The Cato Handbook for Congress* (Washington: Cato Institute, 1995), pp. 253–63. See also Fred L. Smith Jr.

and Kent Jeffreys, "A Free-Market Environmental Vision," in *Market Liberalism: A Paradigm for the 21st Century* (Washington: Cato Institute, 1993), pp. 389–402.

86. Congress should also nullify the old maxim that ignorance of the law is no excuse. See Timothy Lynch, "Ignorance of the Law: Sometimes a Valid Defense," *Legal Times*, April 4, 1994, p. 22.

87. Pennsylvania has protected its citizens from overzealous prosecutors with such a law for many years. See 1 Pa.C.S.A. 1208.

88. See *United States v. Freezo Brothers, Inc.*, 602 F.2d 1123, 1125–27 (1979); and *United States v. Phelps Dodge Corporation*, 391 F. Supp. 1181, 1183 (1975), in which a similar enforcement approach advocated by Sen. Edmund Muskie (D-Maine) and Rep. William H. Harsha (R-Ohio) is cited.

4. HIPAA and the Criminalization of American Medicine

Grace-Marie Turner

Waste, fraud, and abuse in federal health care programs are serious problems, but so are the federal government's efforts to combat them. There are egregious cases of fraud, and those engaged in these criminal activities should be stopped and prosecuted. But an expanding dragnet for "health care criminals" is threatening and intimidating innocent doctors as well. It is creating an unhealthy climate of fear and defensiveness that is having an adverse impact on the medical profession.

In its zeal to rid the nation's health care system of waste, fraud, and abuse, Congress has passed a blizzard of new federal criminal provisions targeting the health care industry, including those contained in the Health Insurance Portability and Accountability Act (HIPAA) of 1996. Congress created new "health care" laws on top of the existing mountain of rules and regulations and funded an army of enforcement agents. The statutes are being enforced by hundreds of federal agents, armed with hundreds of millions of dollars in investigatory funds. This new army of law enforcement agents has been sweeping through hospitals and doctors' offices throughout the country to investigate a new class of "health care offenders."

Mark L. Bennett Jr., an attorney with the firm of Bennett & Dillon, L.L.P., in Topeka, Kansas, says that health care has become the prosecution of choice for many U.S. attorneys: "At one point in time, drugs and drug offenders got the most attention from the authorities, then it was banking and savings and loan violations. Now . . . one of the prosecutions of choice is fraud relating to the provision of medical services. . . . That's where the money is."[1]

The federal government uses the threat of prosecution and arbitrary penalties to collect excessive settlements from doctors "guilty" of clerical errors. Federal officials have developed a crude system to extrapolate fines on doctors and hospitals. Any billing practice that establishes a physician as a financial outlier on a computer statistical analysis can lead to a payment audit. The audit may look at a fraction of the doctor's medical records, identify a percentage that have coding or billing errors, and then extrapolate the estimated overbillings to the whole practice on the basis of the sample. But Medicare enforcement officials do not stop there—they then may impose penalties as great as *three times* the total amount of those estimated overbillings.[2]

Many of the nation's 650,000 physicians are living in fear that they could face armed federal agents, prosecution, and even jail time because of the dangerous new trend of criminalizing the practice of medicine. "Demonizing the entire medical community with the broad brush of 'fraud, waste and abuse' trivializes real fraud and sets up an adversarial tension in every patient-physician encounter," according to Nancy Dickey, M.D., former president of the American Medical Association.[3]

HIPAA Loads New Bullets into Enforcement Guns

The national effort to target medical professionals began in earnest when the Clinton administration introduced the concept of "health care offenses" into the general public lexicon in its proposed 1993 Health Security Act. Although the public rejected the bill within less than one year, many of its enforcement provisions became law two years later as part of the Health Insurance Portability and Accountability Act of 1996, sponsored by Senators Edward Kennedy (D-Mass.) and Nancy Kassebaum (R-Kan.). To the surprise of strong critics of the original Clinton health plan, congressional staff resurrected nearly identical language from many of the enforcement provisions in the 1993 Clinton bill and transplanted them into the Kennedy-Kassebaum legislation.

HIPAA broke ground in creating a new national health care fraud and abuse control program to coordinate federal, state, and local law enforcement efforts. It also created a federal criminal statute specific to health care offenses, making it easier for authorities to prosecute. It provided generous funding for authorities to investigate and prosecute violators, and instituted a fraud and abuse data collection program in which government agencies and health plans are required to report on "final adverse actions" against providers.[4]

Federal Health Care Offenses

HIPAA defines a "federal health care offense" as a violation of, or a conspiracy to violate, any of the nine current criminal statutes or any of the four new health care crimes created under the act: health care fraud, embezzlement, false statements, and obstruction.

The penalties for health care fraud are even more onerous than a similar provision contained in the Clinton Health Security Act. Under HIPAA, anyone knowingly and willfully executing a scheme to defraud any health care benefit program or to falsely obtain money or property owned by or under the control of any health benefit program faces imprisonment of not more than 10 years, a $250,000 fine, or both. If these schemes result in bodily injury, the person responsible can be imprisoned for 20 years. If the patient dies, a life sentence can be imposed.

HIPAA's broad provision on false statements makes anyone who knowingly and willfully falsifies or covers up material information or makes false statements in connection with the delivery of health care benefits liable for fines, jail terms, or both.

Criteria and penalties for obstruction and embezzlement are similar. One section creates a new penalty for "incorrect coding or medically unnecessary services." There is a separate penalty for a pattern of upcoding.

Conviction on a health care fraud offense under HIPAA can easily lead to a money laundering conviction, according to the Medical Association of Georgia's David A. Cook: "Money laundering occurs when funds gained illegally are commingled with funds earned legitimately."[5] Since physicians usually deposit Medicare and Medicaid checks into their practice accounts, the physician may also face money-laundering charges because he or she commingled allegedly tainted funds with legitimate revenue.

Bounty System for Fraud Enforcement

HIPAA provided two major sources of new funding for federal anti-fraud programs.

The Office of Inspector General (OIG) at the Department of Health and Human Services and the Attorney General jointly run the Fraud and Abuse Control Program. It is funded through a trust account, which in turn is funded by criminal fines, civil judgments, forfeitures, penalties, and damages imposed on health care providers and institutions.

This self-funding mechanism, in which money from this trust then is used to finance more fraud and abuse investigations and prosecutions, was also a provision of the Clinton Health Security Act. Politicians, who did not want to add red ink to the federal budget by adding another spending program, instead created a program in which federal health care authorities have a huge financial incentive to extract settlements and judgments from health care providers. Just as in the Clinton Health Security Act, they can seize property, sell it, and use the money to fund more health care investigators.

In addition, Congress appropriated more than $100 million a year to supplement the account. The FBI received an additional appropriation of $47 million in 1997, increasing to $114 million in 2002, for investigations of health care offenses through the Fraud and Abuse Control Program. HIPAA also created separate funding for a Medicare Integrity Program, enabling investigators to go after alleged violators of Medicare law even more aggressively. Program funding grew from $430 million in 1997 up to $710 million in 2002. The law created a private-sector enforcement force by authorizing the use of private contractors.

Congress has criticized the Health Care Financing Administration (HCFA), recently renamed the Centers for Medicare and Medicaid Services, for not having been aggressive enough in awarding contracts to carry out the activities specified in law, including investigating doctors, auditing cost reports, recovery of payments, education of providers, and so forth. HCFA responded by aggressively stepping up its efforts. HIPAA even created an incentive plan to encourage Medicare beneficiaries and health plan employees to become "whistleblowers" and report information that leads to the collection of at least $100.

Other Sanctions

One of the most ominous provisions of the law allows the government to exclude a provider from federal programs simply on the basis of an indictment or "on OIG-initiated determinations of misconduct, for example, poor quality care or submission of false claims for Medicare or Medicaid payment."[6] This means that a provider need not even have been found guilty to face catastrophic damages.

HIPAA's Health Care Fraud and Abuse Data Collection Program requires publication of judgments against medical providers, suppliers, or others convicted of health care offenses. Any health plan that fails to report "final adverse actions" against any health care professional is subject to fines of up to $25,000 per instance not reported.[7]

The Department of Health and Human Services (HHS) claimed in the explanation of its new rule that "Congress intended a broad interpretation of the terms 'health care fraud and abuse,' . . . including *adverse patient outcomes*, failure to provide covered or needed care in violation of contractual arrangements, or delays in diagnosis and treatment" (emphasis added).[8]

In other words, HHS can use HIPAA to enforce "quality of health care." And doctors and hospitals are not the only ones in the enforcers' sights. HHS has interpreted health care practitioners covered by the statute to include "nurses, chiropractors, podiatrists, emergency medical technicians, physical therapists, pharmacists, clinical psychologists, acupuncturists, dieticians, aides, and licensed or certified alternative medicine practitioners such as homeopaths and naturopaths."[9]

Politicians Duck Hard Choices

Weak Data

Most of HIPAA's fraud and abuse provisions were passed despite the absence of good data on how much fraud and abuse there is, where it is, and how bad it is. Congress was legislating in the dark in 1996, and data on fraud and abuse have improved little since then.

In February 1999, Secretary of Health and Human Services Donna Shalala claimed that government efforts had led to a dramatic decrease in health care fraud and abuse, noting that Medicare's $12.6 billion in erroneous claims in 1998 were down from $20.3 billion in 1997. Yet the audit conducted by the Office of Inspector General at HHS revealed that the declining numbers resulted primarily from a big drop in "documentation errors"—from 44 percent of Medicare overpayments in 1996 compared with 16.8 percent in 1997. The "documentation error" decline made up $8.7 billion of the $10.6 billion reduction in "improper" Part A and B payments.[10]

An example from the audit is illustrative: "A physician was paid $103 for an initial patient consultation, with a comprehensive history, exam, and 'moderate' medical decision-making. It was determined [following an audit] that documentation supported a less complex, problem-focused history and exam and $46 was denied."[11]

As former AMA president Dr. Dickey pointed out, "The government relies on an 'estimate' of improper payments based upon a review of claims that were filed for 600 Medicare patients. That's 0.0015% of Medicare's 39 million beneficiaries. It's from this sample that officials project that $12.6 billion is being ripped off the system."[12] The sample clearly is too small to be accurate.

Many of the errors involve doctors mistakenly failing to put the correct number (drawn from thousands of billing codes) in the right box on the correct form. Nonetheless, HIPAA's new penalties for such clerical errors are stiff: possible fines up to $10,000 for each instance.[13]

Following Uninformed Public Opinion

Congressional policy toward health care fraud and abuse has been fueled by political polls, which were in turn fueled by misinformation and a crude political expediency, or the vague need to "do something" about waste, fraud, and abuse. National polling data consistently show that most Americans erroneously believe that high health care costs are almost exclusively the result of fraud and abuse.

Particularly in the mid- and late 1990s, both Congress and the White House used waste, fraud, and abuse in Medicare as a scapegoat. Rather than tackling the tough job of reforming the program, they implemented the original Clinton plan's punitive regulatory regime. At the same time, political leaders failed to educate the public on the seriousness of Medicare's financial problems. Stopping every instance of fraud and improper billing could not come close to saving Medicare from its looming insolvency.

Why Current Financial Arrangements Invite Fraud

While Congress and the Clinton administration were engaged in a fraud and abuse vendetta, both did an abysmal job of reforming a government system that remains a greenhouse for corruption. Clearly, it is easier for politicians to point fingers at doctors than to blame themselves for the flawed public policies that created the climate for waste in the health care system in the first place.

What is it about Medicare and Medicaid that makes them such a target? The editors of the *New York Times* observed in 1997, "The truth is that the Health Care Financing Administration, the Federal oversight agency for Medicare, has neither the financial means nor the ability to tightly supervise the numbingly complex system."

Medicare's Regulatory Fog

Dr. Robert Waller, chairman emeritus of the Mayo Foundation and former president of the Healthcare Leadership Council, told the National Bipartisan Commission on the Future of Medicare in August 1998 that Medicare's regulatory complexity, rather than widespread fraud in the program, is the real problem.

Waller testified that "Medicare's complexity . . . thousands of pages of regulations, rules, manuals, instructions, letters, alerts, notices, etc. . . . has a negative impact on patient care. It steals time from patient care and scholarship . . . dilutes the value of medical records—changing them from a medical record to a billing and coding record—and . . . breeds mistakes. We must all have zero tolerance for real fraud, but differences in interpretation and honest mistakes are not fraud."[14]

Dr. Waller noted that the number of pages of federal health care rules and regulations his facilities must follow now totals 132,720 pages, the vast majority of which (about 111,000) govern Medicare.[15]

Physicians are increasingly lost in this Medicare fog, confused about what Medicare will or will not pay for in the course of treating patients. They cannot know for sure whether Medicare will pay for a service until after the fact.

The Medical Necessity Mess

Under Medicare, bureaucrats struggle to define the meaning and application of "medically improper or unnecessary health care services."[16] Even among experts, there is disagreement over whether a payment will be withheld over a treatment or procedure, depending on whether or not the Medicare bureaucracy will deem it medically necessary or appropriate. The ultimate decision currently rests with the Secretary of Health and Human Services—not patients and doctors—in deciding what is medically necessary for Medicare patients.

But it is impossible for the federal government to define a term as medically ambiguous as "medical necessity" in a way that would get it right for every patient in every medical circumstance. In the meantime, doctors cannot be sure what the government's definition will be in any given case. Congress should heed these words of caution: If it cannot define the standard to be applied, it should not create new federal crimes.

Examples of this medical "twilight zone" are numerous. Dr. Philip M. Catalano recounts his experience as a Florida dermatologist in trying to treat patients for actinic keratosis, a precancerous skin condition:

> HCFA has decided that only a limited number of actinic keratoses can be frozen within a given period of time. In other words, if a patient with severe sun damage has the upper limit done (now 15 on a single day's session) and comes back in a couple of months with another lesion or two, the subsequent lesions can be rejected by Medicare on the grounds that they "exceed" the limits imposed by Medicare. Interestingly enough, the total number which can be done in a given time period is a secret. . . . Medicare will not tell you, they will only tell you that you exceeded the limits.[17]

To add double jeopardy, the Medicare Private Contracting provision contained in Section 4507 of the Balanced Budget Act of 1997 could forbid the patient from paying the doctor privately to have the skin lesions removed unless the doctor gets out of the Medicare program altogether for two years.

Dr. Philip R. Alpert, a California internist specializing in geriatrics, points to another absurdity of Medicare rules in governing colon cancer screens:

> If a doctor orders a stool specimen to test for occult blood—which might indicate an early colon cancer—is he engaging in good medical practice or criminal behavior? Answer: It depends. If the patient doesn't have symptoms and the bill is sent to Medicare, it's a criminal offense because these preventive services are not covered benefits. Thus, billing them to Medicare is considered fraud. The absence of intent to cheat Medicare doesn't matter. Fines of up to $10,000 per incident of fraud may be levied on the physician who simply orders the test from a lab at no personal profit.[18]

Medicaid's Fraud and Abuse Time Bomb

The problems that plague Medicare plague Medicaid as well. The HHS Office of Inspector General acknowledged in testimony before

Congress in March 1999 that the Health Care Financing Administration had no method for arriving at a national estimate of wrongly paid Medicaid claims in the program that pays for medical care for the poor. Further, Assistant Inspector General Joseph Vengrin said there has been a "fairly substantial" drop-off in site visits and audits of Medicaid providers "over the past few years, at least in part because of a lack of resources."[19]

Because Medicaid is a joint federal-state program, responsibility is diffused. Auditors found that "weaknesses identified in prior years' audits were not corrected" and that there was "significantly reduced emphasis on detecting Medicaid errors and irregularities and on requiring states to devote resources to fraud and abuse collection and activity." Vengrin told Congress the states are reluctant to work with HCFA because there is no mandate for them to do so.[20] While federal officials focus on Medicare, criminals very likely are focusing on Medicaid. It is a fraud-and-abuse time bomb waiting to explode, and it is beginning to get the attention of Congress, which is exploring the possibility of creating a Medicaid Commission to study the program and its problems.

The Real Criminals

Although the great majority of doctors are honest, the structure of the Medicare and Medicaid programs leaves them vulnerable to real criminals. The serious con artists, intent on bilking the Medicare and Medicaid programs and private insurance companies, take great pains to study the rules and find ways around them. They carefully figure out how to create schemes that siphon millions of dollars through fly-by-night health care organizations.

The most common scheme is to create fake companies that seek reimbursement for fictional treatments of real patients by real doctors. Patients and doctors both can be victims, with taxpayers footing the bill. The *New York Times* described one typical fraudulent plot:

> Sham companies are created which, through various schemes, get names and billing numbers for actual patients. The companies then submit claims for the real patients with fictional treatments. As a result, untold numbers of patients can be listed in insurance-company computers without their knowledge, describing ailments they never had and for which they never received treatment. Without their knowledge or authorization, criminals use real doctors' names on

large numbers of phony claims. Once the fraudulent scheme is detected, insurance companies and federal agents begin investigating the innocent doctors and delay payment on their legitimate bills. By then, tax authorities also have then gone after them for evading taxes on income that they never received.[21]

Of course, there is a difference in the powers of government and those of private-sector companies in detecting and combating fraud. "The government can utilize powers not available to private managed care companies; namely, criminal prosecution and forfeiture of assets," says David Cook. He points out that "Because it is so politically unpopular to address beneficiary eligibility and benefits, targeting physicians and other providers becomes an attractive alternative for policy-makers." Not only will reduced payments and the constant threat of criminal and civil sanctions fail to achieve the desired monetary savings, they also will ultimately drive physicians out.[22]

Flawed structures of both the private- and public-sector health insurance programs—where the distance between doctors and patients is lengthened by the intervention of complex third-party payment systems—invite fraud, abuse, and mistakes. But rather than begin to fix the complex systems that create a climate for fraudulent schemes, politicians instead have opted to impose a wide-ranging regulatory scheme that covers all doctors and hospitals in hopes they will catch some of the criminals. While this dragnet for criminals ensnares innocent doctors in a dizzying web of paperwork, commonsense principles of public policy have yet to be employed in the serious business of reducing fraud in the Medicare and Medicaid programs.

"The basic system seems designed to enable fraud," former AMA president Daniel (Stormy) Johnson, M.D., told this author. "Why not be on the side of trying to get this fixed rather than throwing hundreds of millions of dollars at these investigations?"

The Big Business of Fraud Enforcement

The current regulatory regime is breeding a whole new industry of billing consultants, administrative specialists, technocrats, and experts on Medicare law, rules, and regulations, including lawyers and insurance agents. Among the most well-attended sessions at the American Bar Association's recent meetings have been those devoted to representing doctors in fraud investigations. Given the current career-ruining regime of Medicare regulation, that's hardly surprising.

Medical malpractice insurance now routinely covers the cost of investigations. In Wisconsin, for example, the largest medical malpractice insurer has added a new benefit to policies for doctors. If the doctors have fraud compliance programs in place in their offices, they can get $25,000 in coverage to cover the costs of a fraud investigation. The insurance company, PIC Wisconsin, said it added the benefit because "there's been a lot of activity by feds who are looking for ways to investigate and uncover billing errors."[23]

"The fear of investigations is so great among physicians that many of them have begun to submit reduced bills to Medicare in case they are audited," Wisconsin physician Sandra Mahkorn told me.

One private company is using doctors' fear of investigations as part of its marketing plan. The company disguised its marketing materials as a threatening notice from the government. The marketing letter is headlined "Fraud & Abuse Compliance Alert." It looks like a letter from a government agency and is stamped "Second Notice." The letter offers a 900-page *Fraud and Abuse Answer Book* to "explain government rules and enforcement actions in plain English." It says it provides "the most current information" on "Stark II, the Anti-Kickback Statute, HIPAA, the Balanced Budget Act, Operation Restore Trust, the False Claims Act, OIG model compliance plans and more." Further, the letter says the book "reveals how the government goes about investigating providers and furnishes crucial information on your rights."

Nonprofits are in the game as well: The National Health Care Anti-Fraud Association (NHCAA) offers a series of training programs and "provides leading-edge information on health care fraud prevention, detection, investigation, and prosecution techniques to approximately 1,000 anti-fraud professionals representing private health payers' special investigation units and public-sector law enforcement and health care administration personnel."[24]

Turning Senior Citizens Loose on Their Doctors

Making matters worse, on top of the complex and detailed regulatory environment in which physicians are forced to operate under the existing Medicare law, Congress enacted a bounty hunter provision in HIPAA, which pays senior citizens for helping to ferret out fraud. The leadership of the AARP, a powerful interest group supporting health policy initiatives for seniors, sought to capitalize on the public's anti-fraud sentiment. After HIPAA was enacted, AARP launched an effort to turn Medicare patients into informers by providing them with a "Medicare Fraud Fighters Kit," composed of a magnifying glass and highlighter, pen, notepad, bumper sticker, and a refrigerator magnet listing the fraud-fighting 800 number. The tacit assumption is that Medicare patients will understand Medicare billing rules better than Medicare doctors. Seniors become eligible for the bounties if information on improper billing by their doctors uncovers abuses.

Jane Orient, M.D., executive director of the Association of American Physicians and Surgeons, warned, "We hope the government will reconsider the cynical use of seniors as paid informants. Seniors may not realize a phone call to the government fraud hot line could unleash a chain of events that could destroy their doctors."[25] Adds former AMA president Johnson, "Professional liability already says anyone who walks in the door is a potential threat to your practice" [because of medical liability]. Now, everyone over 65 is a potential whistleblower" for federal enforcement agents, he told me.

Doctors at Risk

Civil actions have become lucrative for law enforcement agencies (see Table 1). The government can seek $10,000 in fines for each violation, plus three times the amount of the charges in question. One dispute over $50,000 in Medicare bills wound up in a court with fines and penalties totaling $15 million.[26] In this legal climate, doctors fear their livelihoods and financial security are at risk if their office assistants happen to make errors on federal forms. Even if they can withstand the financial losses, doctors are particularly terrified of reputation-ruining fraud charges. They often feel it is safer to simply pay heavy fines than to fight the federal government.

For example, one physician, who feared having his name used, was challenged by federal authorities on a Medicare bill.[27] He did not think that the service he provided to his patient was "covered" under Medicare rules. However, he called program administrators, and he was told that it was a covered service. He soon was paid by

Table 1
FRAUD AND ABUSE COLLECTIONS

	1997	1998	1999	2000	2001
Judgments, settlements, fines (millions of dollars)	$1,200[a]	$480	$524	$1,200	$1,700
Criminal indictments filed	282	322	371	457	445
Convictions	363	326	396	467	465
Civil cases pending	4,010	3,471	2,278	1,995	1,746
Civil cases filed	89	107	91	233	188
Exclusions from Medicare/Medicaid	1,000	3,021	2,976	3,350	3,756

[a]More than $500 million of this amount resulted from settlements in three cases involving clinical laboratory billing practices.

SOURCE: Department of Health and Human Services and Department of Justice, Health Care Fraud and Abuse Control Program, Annual Reports for FY 1997, 1998, 1999, 2000, and 2001.

Medicare, but officials later changed their minds, saying that the service was not covered after all. The physician was required to reimburse Medicare. He complained and soon found federal investigators in his office demanding to audit his entire practice.

How the Regulatory Regime Impacts Patients

For nearly two decades, political leaders have been tightening the screws on health care providers in the belief that they can penalize providers and cut payments without any impact on patients. In their efforts to get control of mushrooming costs, politicians have tried to insulate beneficiaries. However, the changes ultimately cannot help but impact patients. The government increasingly is inserting itself between the physician and the patient in the most intimate decisions involving medical care. The consequences are serious.

Compromising Patient Care

Because doctors increasingly are forced to practice medicine by the bureaucratic book to avoid possible prosecutions, they are less likely to be innovative and to offer newer treatments that have not yet been approved by the regulators. Among other things, says Dr. Waller, the "blizzard of Medicare billing rules . . . has a negative

85

impact on quality of medical care, research, and education, as it steals time from direct care of the patient, from new technology development, and other scholarly activities that lead to new discoveries in diagnosis and treatment of illness."[28]

Doctors who are buried in government paperwork are not spending time increasing their medical knowledge. Instead, they have to devote more and more time to paperwork exercises. For example, a prominent newsletter advertised a conference for anesthesiologists in the summer of 1999 that was entitled "Anesthesia Billing, Coding & Compliance 1999." Sadly, anesthesiologists have a higher stake in attending such events to make sure they are not running afoul of health care laws than they do in attending a continuing medical education event on the latest advances in anesthesiology technology.

As an entire industry of consultants and paperwork specialists grows up around the bureaucratic Medicare system, the bureaucracy and its resulting paperwork are increasingly expensive and wasteful. Doctors and hospitals ultimately must pass the costs on to the public, either through higher taxes due to increased spending on federal programs or through higher health insurance costs for those in the private sector.

Doctors are getting divorced from the practice of medicine and married to the public- and private-sector bureaucracies that pay their bills. They are forced to jump through an increasingly complex array of federal hoops that prescribe what they can and cannot do for their patients. They order tests and treatments they otherwise would not—or withhold them—not on the basis of what is best for the patient but on what Medicare will approve for payment (and will not assign for prosecution as "fraud"). The individuality of the patient's needs is lost in the government's ever more aggressive effort to force everyone into the same one-size-fits-all box. Physicians are finding it harder and harder to work in small practices, and they are forming and joining larger groups, which offer greater legal protection but less continuity with their patients.

As attorney Jonathan Emord points out, this is "hastening the arrival of the day when physicians will be able to practice only if they are affiliated with large hospitals or managed care groups that can afford the risk managers, accountants, and lawyers needed to ensure compliance with Medicare regulations."[29]

Clinton Care on the Installment Plan

Among the many elements of the failed Clinton Health Security Act that shocked the public were its onerous enforcement provisions. The 1,342-page bill provided a cornucopia of fines and prison sentences targeting physicians, health plan employees, lawyers, pharmaceutical companies, medical suppliers, and even patients. However, these enforcement provisions were integral to a health care system that was designed by government to force everyone to play by the same set of rules. In such a system, escape hatches must be closed.

One of the biggest concerns the American people had about the Clinton bill was that government, not doctors, would decide what kind of medical care they should get. With nearly half of the nation's health care bill now being financed through government programs, it already is clear that most of those in the medical profession must comply with government's rules.

The teeth behind those rules can be found in the multitude of criminal and civil statutes that have been enhanced by HIPAA to target health care offenses. Law enforcement agents have powerful weapons to go after health care crime, but their indiscriminate use may harm innocent health care providers and their patients instead.

What Members of Congress Should Do

Americans live in an era of decentralization driven by technology and information dispersal, yet the health care system, both in the public and private sectors, is lumbering along in the opposite direction. Centralized bureaucracies, both public and private, are trying to gain greater and greater control over the most minute aspects of physician-patient encounters. At some point, this effort at centralization will implode.

Under the current system, the enforcement provisions that doctors are complaining about today will only get worse. Penalties are inevitable in any program that attempts to force everyone—patients and doctors—to abide by the same set of rules. The result is a progressive loss of individual freedom. Treating doctors like criminals also cannot help but erode the quality of the medical profession.

Politicians are more than willing to point the finger at fraud and abuse rather than tackle the difficult questions involved in making structural reforms to public and private health care financing systems. Government bureaucracies have churned out thousands of pages of new regulations that are unlikely to stop professional criminals, but that burden average doctors and make honest compliance mistakes even more likely. Many of the problems with health care crime are endemic to the third-party payment system. They would be minimized if basic structural reforms put consumers back in charge in a vibrant, competitive marketplace.

No one is suggesting that patients should be negotiating with doctors for their fees if they are laid out on a stretcher in an emergency room. But savvy American consumers, both working people and senior citizens, are perfectly capable of making decisions about the kind of private insurance arrangements they prefer in case of such an emergency, or even for routine treatment. By being closer to the cost of the insurance policy, consumers inevitably will pay more attention to the cost of the health care they receive. However, achieving that requires structural reform of the health care financing systems in both the private and public sectors to put consumers in charge of resources and choices. The only way to right the system over the long term is to decentralize its financing to allow consumers to have greater control, authority, and responsibility over resources and decisions.

Defederalize Health Care Crime

As former attorney general Edwin Meese III and his colleagues concluded in an American Bar Association Task Force report,[30] enactment of federal offenses that duplicate state laws is not only unnecessary and unwise, but it also has harmful implications for the whole criminal justice system:

> For most of this nation's history, federal criminal jurisdiction was limited to offenses that involved truly national matters, such as treason, counterfeiting, bribery of federal officials, and perjury in the federal courts. But in recent years . . . we federalize everything that walks, talks, and moves.

Congress should return responsibility for criminal investigations and prosecutions to the level of government where it belongs—the states.

Protect Doctors from Wrongful Government Actions

Congress should also put safeguards into place to protect innocent providers from overly aggressive enforcement agents. As Jonathan

Emord observes, "Under HIPAA, health care practitioners may be forced to spend tens of thousands of dollars, lose financial opportunities and their reputations, and yet not be able to recover damages when they are finally proven innocent of wrongdoing."[31] Physicians who are proven innocent should have a statutory right to recoup the money they have lost as a result of wrongful investigations, audits, and enforcement actions. If a doctor or medical facility, following an investigation, has been found not guilty, the government should reimburse all of the costs associated with the legal investigation and actions that may follow.

Eliminate Medicare's Bounty Hunting System

The bounty system enacted in HIPAA creates a trust fund into which money and proceeds from the sale of confiscated property are deposited. The revenues in this trust are then used to finance more fraud and abuse investigations and prosecutions. This self-funding mechanism encourages a quota system in which agents go after citizens to meet their targets to perpetuate funding for their agencies. According to Emord:

> Rewarding those who enforce Medicare fraud and abuse regulations with more program funds creates strong institutional incentives for those enforcers to pursue as many investigations and fraud and abuse prosecutions as possible, thus increasing the risk that the innocent as well as the guilty will suffer punishment. An analogy can be made with the Internal Revenue Service. Past years have brought to light IRS abuses that resulted from agents being rewarded for how much money they could extort from taxpayers. Thus, while the IRS is supposedly abandoning a system of perverse incentives, Congress has mandated such a system for Medicare.[32]

That system should be eliminated.

Apply IRS Audit Reform Standards to Federal Health Care Audits

Many doctors fear criticizing the Centers for Medicare and Medicaid Services (CMS) and other federal fraud and abuse enforcement agencies, or their policies. That fear should be put to rest. If any federal official conducts an audit because of doctor complaints about federal policies, then the legal sanctions that currently govern IRS audits should apply to those federal audits as well. Politically moti-vated or retaliatory audits are a felony under IRS law. They should be a felony under Medicare law, too.

Conclusion

Real change in the American health care system will come only when the power to make health care decisions is taken away from politicians, bureaucrats, lawyers, consultants, and accountants, and placed into the hands of those whose lives and health depend on access to quality medical treatment. More aggressive oversight may make a difference in combating fraud and abuse. But it will come at the cost of further corrosion of the doctor-patient relationship. Every action taken by a doctor or hospital will increasingly be subject to second-guessing and third-party monitoring. Medical judgments made and services rendered will become, in retrospect, grounds for civil and criminal action. Even today, doctors and hospitals practice the art of medicine with the knowledge that even an honest billing error could set off a chain of events that could threaten their liveli-hoods and result in a prison sentence.

To paraphrase Friedrich Hayek, the Nobel Prize-winning econo-mist, there are only two ways of holding men accountable: prices and prisons. Unfortunately, some of the people who get thrown in jail may have honestly misunderstood the regulation they needed to follow.[33] This is not a health care system befitting America.

This is an abridged version of an article originally published in The Cato Journal, *vol. 22, no. 1, Spring/Summer 2002.*

Notes

1. Mark L. Bennett, "Criminal Prosecutions for Medicare and Medicaid Fraud," Association of American Physicians and Surgeons, 1998, www.aapsonline.org/fraud/fraud.htm, p. 1.

2. For example, if federal authorities were to audit a practice, they would analyze a sample of a practitioner's patient charts. Let's say they looked at 25 charts and found errors in 10 of them. That means there were errors in 40 percent of the charts. Then they have to determine how much the errors cost. Let's say they determined that in the 10 erroneous charts the physician had overbilled Medicare by a total of $300, or an average of $30 per chart. To extrapolate the full fine, federal officials next would ask the doctor how many patients he has. If the doctor has 1,000 patients, and Medicare investigators discovered "errors" in 40 percent of the sampled charts, they would assume that there would be errors in 400 of them. They then would multiply the average overbilling amount ($30) by 400 to come up with their estimate

of the total amount of overbillings: $12,000. At that point, "The OIG may impose an assessment, where authorized . . . of not more than three times the amount claimed for each item or service which was a basis for the penalty" (64 *Federal Register,* No. 140, July 22, 1999, p. 39429). That means our doctor could be fined $36,000 on the basis of 10 erroneous charts.

3. Nancy Dickey, "Government to Grandpa: Rat Out Your Doctor," *Wall Street Journal,* February 24, 1999.

4. 42 USC Sec. 1320a-7e.

5. David A. Cook, "Fraud, Abuse, and Beyond: Costly Pitfalls for Physicians Who Serve Medicare and Medicaid Patients." Medical Association of Georgia, August 29, 1997, www.mag.org/content_legal/legal_news_1997_cook_paper.html, p. 7.

6. 67 *Federal Register,* No. 52, March 18, 2002, p. 11928.

7. 63 *Federal Register,* No. 210, October 30, 1998, p. 58347.

8. Ibid., p. 58342.

9. Ibid, p. 58344.

10. *Part B News,* "Prepay Reviews Take a Starring Role in Annual OIG Audit of HCFA," February 15, 1999, p. 1.

11. *Part B News,* "Prepay Reviews Take a Starring Role in Annual OIG Audit of HCFA," February 15, 1999, p. 4.

12. Dickey, "Government to Grandpa: Rat Out Your Doctor."

13. 42 USC Sec. 1320a-7a (civil monetary penalties for "incorrect coding or medically unnecessary services").

14. Robert Waller, "Administration of the Medicare Program," Testimony before the National Bipartisan Commission on the Future of Medicare, August 10, 1998, Washington, D.C.

15. Letter from Bruce M. Kelly, Director of Government Relations, Mayo Foundation, March 4, 1999. "Medicare regulations and supporting documents." The 132,720 pages of rules include Medicare legislation and regulation, fraud and abuse regulation, the Balanced Budget Act of 1997, HCFA manuals, HCFA *Federal Register* pages, carrier manuals, coding manuals, carrier newsletters, intermediary communications, intermediary Medicare bulletins, HCFA administrator decisions, and nearly three dozen other document sets.

16. "Congress intended a broad interpretation of the terms 'health care fraud and abuse' . . . we believe that include(s), . . . services . . . that are medically unnecessary" (63 *Federal Register,* No. 210, October 30, 1998, pp. 58341–42).

17. Philip M. Catalano, Letter to Dr. Robert Moffit, the Heritage Foundation, September 9, 1998.

18. Philip Alpert, "Free Doctors from Medicare's Shackles," *Wall Street Journal,* November 5, 1997, p. A21.

19. Faulkner and Gray, Inc., "There's No Way for Feds to Estimate Amount of Error in Medicaid Overpayments." *Medicine & Health,* March 29, 1999.

20. Ibid., 1999b.

21. Kurt Eichenwald, "Unwitting Doctors and Patients Exploited in a Vast Billing Fraud," *New York Times,* February 6, 1998, p. A1.

22. Cook, "Fraud, Abuse, and Beyond," p. 2.

23. Joe Manning, "Insurance Firms Cover Doctors' Legal Fees." *Milwaukee Journal Sentinel,* October 19, 1998, p. 8.

24. NHCAA 2002.

25. Faulkner and Gray, Inc., "Doctors Decry 'Cynical' Uses of Medicare Beneficiaries to Spot Fraud." *Medicine & Health*, March 1, 1999.

26. Michael Pretzer, "What Washington Plans for Doctors," *Medical Economics* 73(7) (1996): 57.

27. Fear among physicians is growing to the point that few physicians would allow this author to use their names for this article.

28. Robert Waller, "Astray in the Medicare Fraud Fog," *Washington Times*, August 12, 1998.

29. Jonathan Emord, "Murder by Medicare," *Regulation* 21 (1998): 31.

30. Edwin Meese, "The Dangerous Federalization of Crime," *Wall Street Journal*, February 22, 1999, p. A19.

31. Emord, op. cit., p. 37.

32. Ibid., p. 32.

33. Citizens Against Government Waste, "Medicare Fraud: The Symptoms and the Cure," Washington, D.C., www.cagw.org/uploads/medicare.pdf, 1997, p. 27.

5. There Goes the Neighborhood: The Bush-Ashcroft Plan to "Help" Localities Fight Gun Crime

Gene Healy

Speaking before the National Governors Association soon after his inauguration, President George W. Bush declared—

> I'm going to make respect for federalism a priority in this administration. Respect for federalism begins with an understanding of its philosophy. The framers of the Constitution did not believe in an all-knowing, all-powerful federal government. They believed that our freedom is best preserved when power is dispersed. That is why they limited and enumerated the federal government's powers and reserved the remaining functions of government to the states.[1]

Unfortunately, "respect for federalism" is too often honored in the breach, rather than in the observance. And that has been the case with the Bush administration's crime-control strategy, which flies in the face of the Tenth Amendment and the doctrine of enumerated powers.

The centerpiece of President Bush's crime-fighting program is an initiative called Project Safe Neighborhoods, which calls for escalating enforcement of gun control laws. Under the program, many firearm offenses that would ordinarily be prosecuted in state court—such as possession of a handgun by a felon or a drug user—are now to be diverted to the federal court system in which mandatory minimum sentences, tougher bond requirements, and the fact that convicts often serve their time out of state are said to provide harsher deterrents. Project Safe Neighborhoods will cost taxpayers more than $550 million over a two-year period by, among other things, hiring more than 700 new lawyers to serve as full-time gun offense prosecutors. According to President Bush, the message of Project

Safe Neighborhoods is "If you use a gun illegally, you will do hard time."[2]

Project Safe Neighborhoods has its roots in Project Exile, an initiative begun in 1997 by federal prosecutors in Richmond, Virginia, and subsequently embraced by many other jurisdictions. Praise of the Project Exile program, which, like the Project Safe Neighborhoods program involves diverting state-level gun prosecutions to federal court, has come from diverse quarters. People who are normally at odds with one another over gun control—such as Sarah Brady, Charlton Heston, Sen. Charles Schumer (D-N.Y.), and Attorney General John Ashcroft—have lauded Exile for its supposedly tough-minded approach to crime.[3]

Agreement among people of disparate viewpoints might be taken to indicate the reasonableness of the Bush initiative, but a closer look at Safe Neighborhoods and Exile reveals that such programs are an affront to the constitutional principle of federalism. Moreover, such initiatives will likely lead to overenforcement of gun laws and allow prosecutors to select their preferred forum—federal or state—on the basis of the racial composition of the respective jury pools. As the constitutional and policy implications of Project Safe Neighborhoods and Project Exile emerge, the Bush initiative looks less like a commonsense solution to crime and more like a political gimmick with pernicious unintended consequences.

The Genesis of Project Safe Neighborhoods

Exile on Main Street

Project Exile, the prototype for President Bush's Project Safe Neighborhoods, began in Richmond in 1997, when an ambitious federal prosecutor, David Schiller, started aggressively prosecuting handgun offenses that would normally have been handled in state courts. At that time, Richmond suffered disproportionately from violent crime, routinely landing a spot among the 10 cities with the highest per capita murder rates.[4] Schiller took it upon himself to try to reduce that rating. As Schiller described his strategy, under Project Exile, "all felons with guns, guns/drug cases and guns/domestic violence cases in Richmond are federally prosecuted, without regard to numbers or quantities."[5] The billboards advertising the program along Interstate 95 put it concisely: "An Illegal Gun Gets You Five Years in Federal Prison."

Helen Fahey, then-U.S. attorney for the Eastern District of Virginia and Schiller's boss, describes Exile as being "named for the idea that if the police catch a criminal in Richmond with a gun, the criminal has forfeited his right to remain in the community.... [He] will be 'exiled' to federal prison."[6] From Fahey and Schiller's perspective, there were several distinct advantages to bringing firearm cases in federal court. First, federal bond statutes would allow most offenders to be held without bail. Second, offenders prosecuted in federal court would be subject to mandatory minimum sentences under federal law, resulting in stiff penalties. Finally, according to Fahey, "Defendants know that a federal jail term will likely be served elsewhere in the country. This has a major impact because serving a jail sentence among friends ... is seen by defendants as much less onerous than serving time in a prison out of state."[7]

To further their goal of getting guns off Richmond's streets, Schiller and Fahey helped assemble a coalition of business and community leaders that eventually became the Project Exile Citizen Support Foundation. That foundation raised money for radio ads, billboard space, and a city bus painted black and bearing the warning that illegal possession of a gun brings with it a five-year term in federal prison.[8] The NRA contributed $125,000 to Richmond's advertising programs.[9]

Exile featured extensive cooperation between local and federal officials. Each Richmond police officer was given a 24-hour pager number for an on-call agent from the Bureau of Alcohol, Tobacco and Firearms and cue cards listing federal gun possession crimes.[10] Richmond police were directed to pursue suspects for, among other offenses, carrying a weapon while possessing drugs, being a convicted felon in possession of a weapon, and being an illegal alien in possession of a weapon—all federal crimes.[11]

By March 1999, two years after Exile's inception, 512 guns had been seized, and federal prosecutors had secured 438 indictments and 302 convictions with an average sentence of more than 53 months.[12] Other federal prosecutors followed Schiller and Fahey's lead; the program was expanded to the Norfolk and Tidewater areas of Virginia as well as Rochester, New York. Philadelphia, Oakland, Birmingham, and Baton Rouge are also implementing their own versions of Project Exile.[13]

Congressional Republicans took notice of Exile and praised its hard-line approach to the enforcement of existing gun laws. In April

2000 the House of Representatives passed Rep. Bill McCollum's (R-Fla.) Project Exile Act, which would have provided $100 million in federal funds for Exile programs across the country.[14] Presidential candidate George W. Bush touted Exile on the campaign trail and called for nationwide expansion of the program along the lines proposed by the House.[15]

The Bush-Ashcroft Program

Making good on his campaign promise, in May 2001 President Bush unveiled his anti-crime initiative, Project Safe Neighborhoods, which uses Project Exile as its model. The program would "take Exile national," bringing to cities all across America what David Schiller brought to Richmond. Safe Neighborhoods' centerpiece is a plan to hire a host of new federal prosecutors, dedicated to bringing federal gun charges for offenses that would normally be handled in state courts. The Bush proposal would fund 113 new assistant U.S. attorneys to serve as full-time gun prosecutors.[16]

Safe Neighborhoods also aims to promote gun prosecutions at the state and local levels. In addition to the funds for new federal prosecutors, the president's proposal dedicates $75 million to hiring and training full-time state and local prosecutors. That money is expected to fund around 600 new gun prosecutors.[17] Other funding will be available through Project Safe Neighborhoods to "coordinate all gun-related programs," including community outreach programs, but Safe Neighborhoods' central goal is to raise the number of firearm offense prosecutions in America. As the president put it in his remarks announcing the program, "This Nation must enforce the gun laws which exist on the books."[18]

Constitutional Federalism and Crime

President Bush's concern with violent crime is understandable, and his desire to tackle the problem without adding to the gun laws already on the books is laudable. But as Bush himself would acknowledge, good intentions are not enough; reformers must operate within the bounds of our Constitution—a charter that divides powers and responsibilities between the federal and the state governments.

Is Project Safe Neighborhoods consistent with the "respect for federalism" that President Bush professes? To answer that question, it is necessary to review the constitutional framework for federal criminal law.

The Original Design

As President Bush recognized in his remarks to the governors, the Constitution's enumeration of the federal government's powers was meant to limit the reach of the federal government. The only powers the federal government possesses are those that have been delegated to it by the people and enumerated in the Constitution. All other powers are, as the Tenth Amendment confirms, "reserved to the states respectively, or to the people."

The Constitution provides the federal government with an exceedingly slender grant of authority over criminal law. There are three specifically enumerated federal crimes—counterfeiting, piracy, and treason—and two general founts of federal criminal authority—Congress's power to punish "offenses against the law of nations" and its power to "make all laws which shall be necessary and proper for carrying into Execution the foregoing Powers."

The records of the Constitutional Convention indicate that the federal role in criminal law was limited by design. At the Philadelphia Convention, discussion of criminal law issues focused almost exclusively on treason, piracy, counterfeiting, and offenses against the law of nations.[19] Federal criminal authority, like federal authority in general, was to be directed in the main toward affairs of state and international relations, as well as protecting the federal government and its interests. As James Madison noted in Federalist Paper no. 45—

> The powers delegated by the proposed Constitution to the federal government are few and defined. Those which are to remain in the State governments are numerous and indefinite. The former will be exercised principally on external objects, such as war, peace, negotiation, and foreign commerce. . . . The powers reserved to the several states will extend to all objects which, in the ordinary course of affairs, concern the lives, liberties, and properties of the people, and the internal order, improvement, and prosperity of the State.[20]

Alexander Hamilton agreed that criminal laws were the province of the states and argued that this would help the states maintain the affections of the citizenry and resist encroachments by the federal government:

> There is one transcendent advantage belonging to the province of the State governments which alone suffices to place the matter in a clear and satisfactory light. I mean the ordinary administration of criminal and civil justice.[21]

Early federal practice hewed closely to that understanding. The first Congress enacted the Crimes Act of 1790, which established 17 federal criminal offenses. For the most part, the Crimes Act was directed at ends unquestionably federal in nature—interference with the federal government and its operations. For example, the act proscribed perjury in federal court, theft of government property, revenue fraud, treason, and bribery of federal officials. Except in areas where the federal government had exclusive jurisdiction, as in the District of Columbia, federal territories, and military bases, early federal criminal law did not reach crimes against individuals, such as murder and ordinary theft.[22]

The Creeping Expansion of Federal Criminal Law

In the post–Civil War era, Congress began to expand into areas traditionally within the ambit of the states' police powers. In response to both state and private violence against the freedmen in the South, Congress enacted a number of civil rights statutes that provided for federal prosecution of certain violations of the freedmen's rights.[23] In addition, the increasing integration of the national economy during the late 19th century provided further impetus for the federalization of crime, in the form of the first mail fraud statute (1872), the criminal provisions of the Interstate Commerce Commission Act (1887), and the Sherman Antitrust Act (1890).

The federal war on alcohol, which began in 1919, also greatly increased the number of federal prosecutions. Despite the fact that Prohibition was repealed in 1933, federalization of crime continued to increase, due in large part to an increasing number of regulatory crimes and a newly expansive interpretation of Congress's power to regulate interstate commerce, sanctioned by the Supreme Court.[24]

But the real surge in the federalization of crime has come over the last 30 years as Congress has ramped up the drug war and increasingly involved itself in the punishment of intrastate acts of violence. According to a report published by the American Bar Association, more than 40 percent of the federal criminal provisions enacted since the Civil War have been enacted since 1970.[25] By the early 1990s, there were more than 3,000 federal crimes on the books.[26] Federal criminal statutes once focused principally on crimes affecting federal interests, but today most such statutes proscribe conduct that is already covered by state criminal law. In 1997, for example, 95 percent of federal prosecutions involved federal statutes that duplicate state criminal statutes.[27] Thus, Congress has seen fit to proscribe offenses such as car theft, drive-by shootings, burning a church, and even disrupting a rodeo.[28] Congress's penchant for involving itself in matters so clearly local and intrastate as those was merely one indication that in the post–New Deal era the federal government had slipped its constitutional moorings.

Project Safe Neighborhoods: A Frontal Assault on Federalism

When the Republican Party won historic majorities in the Senate and House in November 1994, there was good reason to expect that the trend toward overweening federalization had crested and that the distinction between what was properly federal and what was properly local would once again be respected. Republican candidates for the House in that election tried to take advantage of a burgeoning Tenth Amendment movement in the country, and their Contract with America included a pledge to end unfunded mandates on states and localities.[29] As then Senate majority leader Robert Dole (R-Kans.) put it in his first speech to the 104th Congress, "If I have one goal for the 104th Congress, it is this: that we will dust off the 10th Amendment. . . . Our guide will be this question: Is this program a basic function of a limited government?"[30] To stress the point, Dole took to carrying a copy of the Tenth Amendment in his coat pocket and taking it out during speeches.

And indeed there were significant victories for the Tenth Amendment during the period of Republican ascendancy. Not least among them was the advent of a Supreme Court jurisprudence that started to take federalism seriously. Perhaps emboldened by the political trends sweeping the country, the Court in 1995 issued a landmark ruling in *United States v. Lopez* that made clear that the long-dormant doctrine of enumerated powers had not lost its vitality.[31] In *Lopez*, the Court struck down as unconstitutional the Gun-Free School

Zones Act, which criminalized gun possession "at a place the individual knows, or has reasonable cause to believe, is a school zone." According to the Court, to allow Congress to invoke the Commerce Power to regulate a matter so quintessentially local and noncommercial would "bid fair to convert congressional authority under the Commerce Clause to a general police power of the sort retained by the states."[32] When *Lopez* was followed by *Printz v. U.S.*,[33] prohibiting Congress from "commandeering" state and local police officers into enforcing the Brady Handgun Violence Prevention Act, and *U.S. v. Morrison*,[34] striking down the civil suit provisions of the Violence against Women Act as improperly directed toward intrastate crime and beyond the scope of the Commerce Power, it became clear that a historic opportunity to restore federalism was at hand.

Still, a true restoration of the proper relationship between the states and the federal government would have to wait until Republicans took the White House—or so supporters of the Tenth Amendment were told. And in January 2001 the heralded event came to pass. Long-suffering constitutionalists finally saw the day when a president who had named Antonin Scalia and Clarence Thomas as his favorite justices and had pledged himself to "make respect for federalism a priority" in his administration assumed office.

Yet any rejoicing on the part of constitutionalists would be premature, to say the least. In several important areas of domestic policy, President Bush's initiatives suggest that, where it counts, political expediency will trump respect for federalism. For instance, it is hard to think of an issue more undeniably local in nature than education. And yet the president's education initiative, signed on January 8, 2002, dramatically increases federal spending on education and mandates state testing of pupils in reading and math.[35] With Project Safe Neighborhoods, respect for the Tenth Amendment has once again yielded to political calculation.

The political calculation of many supporters of Exile and Safe Neighborhoods is that an aggressive effort to "enforce the gun laws on the books" can forestall the gun control lobby's efforts to enact still more gun laws. Unfortunately, in attempting to preserve Second Amendment rights, supporters of Exile and Safe Neighborhoods are conducting a frontal assault on the constitutional principle of federalism.

100

Bush and Rehnquist Court at Cross-Purposes

The Supreme Court has noted that the division of power between the states and the federal governments is

> one of the Constitution's structural protections of liberty. "Just as the separation and independence of the coordinate branches of the Federal Government serve to prevent the accumulation of excessive power in any one branch, a healthy balance of power between the States and the Federal Government will reduce the risk of tyranny and abuse from either front." To quote Madison, . . . "a double security arises to the rights of the people. The different governments will control each other, at the same time that each will be controlled by itself."[36]

To prevent an excessive accumulation of federal power, the Framers refused to grant plenary police power to the federal government; instead, the Constitution grants Congress authority, pursuant to various enumerated powers, to fashion criminal statutes to protect distinctly federal interests. General law enforcement authority— "the ordinary administration of criminal justice," in Hamilton's phrase—is reserved to the states. With *Lopez*, *Printz*, *Morrison*, and other cases, the Rehnquist Court has begun to slowly shift the balance and restore American criminal law to the original understanding.

Exile and Safe Neighborhoods, in contrast, proceed on the assumption that the federal government has general police powers. By employing federal gun possession statutes that rest on a dubious reading of the power to "regulate commerce . . . among the several states," those programs threaten to make the ordinary administration of criminal justice a federal responsibility. More than one federal court has recognized the dangers inherent in such initiatives. In *United States v. Jones* (1999), a federal appeals court called Project Exile "a substantial federal incursion into a sovereign state's area of authority and responsibility."[37] District Judge Robert E. Payne struck a similar note in *United States v. Nathan* (1998): "The federal government has embarked upon a major incursion into the sovereignty of Virginia." According to Judge Payne, the "risk of attenuating the Tenth Amendment" is present even in Project Exile in its current (voluntary) form. Moreover, "carried to its logical extreme [the argument for Exile] would make federal officers responsible for prosecuting all serious crimes in federal courts. Were that the case,

101

we soon would have a federal police force with the attendant risk of the loss of liberty which that presents."[38]

Indeed, the Bush administration, with its embrace of the Exile model, seems bent on obliterating the distinction between what is properly local and what is properly national. One of the initiatives under the Project Safe Neighborhoods umbrella is Project Sentry, which Attorney General Ashcroft describes as "a vital federal-state project dedicated to prosecuting gun crimes committed at our nation's schools and dedicated to protecting juveniles from gun crime."[39] Under Project Sentry, the Justice Department will provide every U.S. Attorney's Office with a new prosecutor to combat "school-related gun violence."[40] A more brazen affront to the Rehnquist Court's landmark ruling in *Lopez*—striking down the Gun-Free School Zones Act—could hardly be imagined. In that case, Congress's attempt to make a federal crime out of gun possession in the vicinity of a school was held to be beyond the limited powers delegated to the federal government. The Court noted that, under the government's theory of the case, "it is difficult to perceive any limitation on federal power, even in areas such as criminal law enforcement or education where States historically have been sovereign."[41] Needless to say, the actions of President Bush do not match his statements with respect to federalism.

Clogging the Courts

Disregarding our constitutional structure, as Exile and Safe Neighborhoods do, brings with it a host of troubling consequences.[42] In 1998 the American Bar Association's Task Force on the Federalization of Criminal Law examined the grave problems caused by promiscuous federalization of crime. Many of the concerns the task force addressed are inherent in Project Exile and the president's Project Safe Neighborhoods. Among those concerns are "the centralization of criminal law enforcement power in the federal government," the threat of "disparate results for the same conduct," "diminution of a principled basis for selecting a case as a federal or local crime," and "increased power at the federal prosecutorial level," leading to less local control of prosecutors.[43]

But perhaps the most immediate danger lies in Project Safe Neighborhoods' "adverse impact on the federal judicial system."[44] Simply put, the federal government's primary responsibility is to provide a legal forum in which citizens with valid federal claims can promptly and dependably vindicate their rights. Project Safe Neighborhoods' federalization of crime will distract the federal courts by greatly exacerbating the strain on the federal court system—a phenomenon that Chief Justice Rehnquist has repeatedly decried.[45] Mindful of Rehnquist's warnings, Judge Richard L. Williams, chief judge of the U.S. District Court in Richmond, complained in a letter to the chief justice that Project Exile has "transformed [our court] into a minor-grade police court," reducing the amount of time judges can spend on matters that are properly federal.[46]

Judge Williams is right to worry; federal criminal cases do appear to be crowding out complex civil matters. Despite a growing absolute number of civil cases on the federal docket, the number of civil trials has decreased to make way for a growing number of federal criminal cases, often involving run-of-the-mill crimes traditionally handled by the states. Although many of the federal criminal cases involve ordinary street crimes, they consume a disproportionate amount of judicial resources, in part because of federal sentencing procedures.[47]

Judge Fred Motz, chief judge of the U.S. District Court for the District of Maryland in Baltimore, says that Project Safe Neighborhoods could be "devastating" to the federal court system. Given that many gun arrests involve drawn-out evidence suppression hearings, according to Judge Motz, "If these [gun possession] cases flood the federal courts, then it is going to have a tremendous impact." That diversion of federal resources will adversely affect the rights of civil litigants seeking redress in federal court delaying resolution of their claims. As Louisiana State University law professor John S. Baker noted, if Safe Neighborhoods is implemented, then "in some places, if you have a civil case, forget it. It's not going anywhere."[48] Thus, the Bush-Ashcroft program is a perfect illustration of an unintended consequence noted by the Nobel laureate economist Milton Friedman, among others—that when government begins to do what it should not, it ceases to do what it should.

Interfering with State Law Enforcement

Safe Neighborhoods' assault on federalism goes beyond simply increasing the number of federal gun prosecutions; its plan to provide funding for state and local prosecutors should also be deeply troubling to people who understand that with federal money come

103

federal "strings." As noted earlier, the Bush plan includes $75 million for a program that would hire about 600 state and local prosecutors; the funding would be conditioned on those prosecutors pursuing gun law violations full-time. That is a dangerous precedent—one that strikes at the very notion of separate spheres of authority for the state and federal governments. By employing the spending power, Congress can direct the administration of state-level criminal justice in areas where there is absolutely no federal interest. In so doing, Congress can circumvent constitutional limits on its enumerated powers.[49] Indeed, using the tactic approved by the Bush administration in Project Safe Neighborhoods, the federal government could dictate increased prosecution of virtually any crime within the ambit of the states' police powers. As federal funding increases relative to state law enforcement budgets, the danger of creeping federal influence over state priorities will likely increase.

Do the Republican conservatives who support Project Safe Neighborhoods really want that program to become the model for federal anti-crime initiatives in the future? If they do, it is difficult to see any stopping point to the politicization of federal crime policy. The program stands as an open invitation for special interest groups to push their own "prosecution-stimulus" initiatives. Take hate crimes, for example. Why should left-leaning pressure groups stop with the passage of a federal hate crimes act? Following the Safe Neighborhoods model, they can push for several hundred new federal and state prosecutors dedicated to bringing hate crime indictments. Feminists will doubtless push for more prosecutors for sexual assault offenses.[50] Nor is there anything to stop advocates of child welfare from promoting the funding of several hundred full-time state-level child abuse prosecutors. In the past, conservatives have expressed valid concerns about whether overzealous prosecutors have been swept up in the emotional nature of the child abuse issue and ended up incarcerating innocent people; federal subsidization of such prosecutions would increase that risk exponentially.[51]

The Republicans who supported Exile and Safe Neighborhoods as a means of forestalling new gun control legislation have been too clever by half. The principle that they have endorsed not only runs roughshod over the idea that the states ought to be able to set their own prosecutorial priorities, it also fairly begs for those priorities to be set by the most vocal and powerful interest groups in Washington. If the "respect for federalism" President Bush has repeatedly professed is genuine, he must reconsider his support for Project Safe Neighborhoods.[52]

The Closer One Looks, The More Problems One Sees

Federalism issues to one side, it is easy to understand the superficial appeal of Project Safe Neighborhoods. The program has the merit of relying on existing laws, rather than calling for new ones. Moreover, the laws it relies on are targeted at offenders unlikely to get much sympathy from the general public: felons and drug users with guns, in large part. But as with many anti-crime initiatives coming out of Washington, a closer look at the program raises questions. What kinds of cases are Safe Neighborhoods prosecutors likely to bring? What opportunities for prosecutorial mischief might be presented by the program?

Assembly-Line Justice

Unlike an ordinary prosecutor, whose bailiwick covers the gamut of criminal law, a Safe Neighborhoods prosecutor is limited to only one category of criminal charges. Whereas other prosecutors are able to shift their focus to other categories of crime once they have charged the most dangerous defendants in a given category of offense, Safe Neighborhoods prosecutors will be expected to continue prosecuting violations of gun laws. Their incentive will be to keep focusing on the numbers—to continue producing indictments and convictions regardless of merit. That incentive threatens to result in assembly-line justice and overenforcement. The incentive structure that Safe Neighborhoods sets up will lead to the proliferation of "garbage" gun charges—technical violations of firearms statutes on which no sensible prosecutor would expend his energy.[53] Worse, Safe Neighborhoods will likely result in federal and state governments' locking up firearms owners who do not deserve to be in jail.

Federal prosecutors already operate under an incentive structure that forces them to focus on the statistical "bottom line." Statistics on arrests and convictions are the Justice Department's bread and butter. They are submitted to the department's outside auditors, are instrumental in assessing the "performance" of the U.S. Attorneys' Offices, and are the focus of the department's annual report. As George Washington University Law School professor Jonathan Turley puts it, "In some ways, the Justice Department continues to operate under the body count approach in Vietnam. . . . They feel a need to produce a body count to Congress to justify past appropriations and secure future increases."[54]

When this focus on charging and conviction rates is combined with Safe Neighborhoods prosecutors' inability to bring charges under other statutes, overenforcement will be the very likely result. Simply put, not every technical violation of federal or state gun statutes deserves to be prosecuted, particularly where, as is the case on the federal level, convictions will lead to mandatory minimum sentences and substantial jail time. But a Safe Neighborhoods prosecutor likely will not have the luxury of eschewing trivial cases.

And the federal criminal code contains a number of trivial gun offenses that will be useful to any Safe Neighborhoods prosecutor who is anxious to keep his or her numbers up. Should the full power of the federal government really be directed at a defendant who has sold a gun to someone he may have reason to believe is an unlawful user of controlled substances or has been discharged from the Armed Forces under dishonorable conditions?[55] Moreover, as at least one federal court has noted, the provision of the federal criminal code that prohibits gun possession by someone under a restraining order in a domestic dispute allows a defendant to be stripped of his Second Amendment rights and imprisoned without even a factual finding that he has ever threatened anyone with violence.[56] Indeed, it appears that Project Exile already encourages skewed priorities on the part of prosecutors. As federal Judge Richard L. Williams commented on Richmond's Project Exile, "Ninety percent of these [Exile] defendants are probably no danger to society."[57]

The same could be said of the defendants incarcerated under Colorado's Project Exile. Reporter David Holthouse examined every Colorado Project Exile prosecution from the program's inception in September 1999 through January 2002. The vast bulk of Colorado Exile defendants were prosecuted under the "prohibited-person-in-possession" statutes (felon, drug user, etc.). Of those defendants, the overwhelming majority—154 of 191—had no violent felonies at all on their records. Two of them were simply illegal aliens without criminal records. Another—in an item picked up by "News of the Weird"–style columns nationwide—went to jail for posing nude with a firearm.[58]

That defendant, a 33-year-old Colorado Springs resident, was arrested when federal authorities came into possession of seven

106

photos of Katica Crippen in various poses, holding a firearm. Her prior drug convictions made her a felon in possession under federal law, and prosecutor James Allison brought the full force of the federal government down on her.

Judge Richard Matsch, who presided over the Oklahoma City bombing trial, was outraged by the poor prosecutorial judgment and the waste of federal resources in the Crippen case. "How far is this policy of locking people up with guns going to go?" Judge Matsch demanded. "I want to know why this is a federal case. Who decided this is a federal crime?"[59]

Fomenting Miscarriages of Justice

More disturbing still is the prospect that Safe Neighborhoods will result in some appalling miscarriages of justice. Consider some of the cases that have been prosecuted in the pre–Project Safe Neighborhoods world.

In April 1999, Brian I. Ford went into a Fairfax City pawnshop to hock a Civil War–era rifle for $35. A few weeks later, thanks to a police background check, Ford was arrested for being a felon in possession of a firearm, because of prior convictions for burglary and robbery. Had the case gone to federal court, Ford would have faced extensive jail time. But because Fairfax did not have a federal Project Exile program, and because Virginia's state-level Exile program had not yet been implemented, the jury was free to recommend only a $1,250 fine and no jail time.[60]

Michael Mahoney wasn't quite so lucky. Mahoney, a Tennessee businessman, is currently serving a 15-year term in federal prison as the result of a minor handgun offense. As the owner of the Hard Rack Pool Hall in Jackson, Tennessee, Mahoney had to make nightly cash deposits at his local bank. He carried a .22-caliber Derringer for personal protection while he did so. When Mahoney's pistol was stolen in 1992, he bought another one at a pawnshop, filling out the background-check form required by federal law. The problem for Mahoney was that 13 years earlier he had been convicted of selling drugs to an undercover police officer three times during the course of a three-week investigation. After the conviction, for which he served 22 months in prison, Mahoney cleaned up his act and became a law-abiding citizen. In 1991 he underwent an extensive background check to get a liquor license. Because he had stayed out of trouble for more than 10 years, the license was granted. Mahoney, wrongly assuming that his lone felony conviction had been wiped out completely, marked down that he was not a felon on the federal background-check form for gun purchases. A BATF investigation resulted in Mahoney's indictment as a convicted felon in possession of a firearm as a result of buying the Derringer in 1991. Under federal mandatory minimum sentencing rules, Mahoney's three drug sales during the 1980 investigation were treated as three separate offenses, making Mahoney a "career criminal" and earning him a minimum sentence of 180 months. Though U.S. District Judge James D. Todd protested that Mahoney's was "not the kind of case that Congress had in mind," his hands were tied by federal law, and he had no choice but to put Mahoney in a jail cell for 15 years.[61]

Safe Neighborhoods promises to put more than 700 full-time gun prosecutors (600 state, 113 federal) to work. Add to that the fact that a job as a full-time gun prosecutor is likely to appeal disproportionately to attorneys with an ideological hostility toward gun ownership and one has the makings of a nationwide "zero tolerance" policy for technical infractions of gun laws. As the program is implemented, one can expect more miscarriages of justice.[62]

Threatening the Right to Trial by Jury

The Sixth Amendment guarantees defendants in "all criminal prosecutions" the right to a public trial "by an impartial jury of the State and district wherein the crime shall have been committed." The Supreme Court has held that the constitutional guarantee of equal protection found in the Fourteenth Amendment and (implicitly) in the Fifth Amendment's Due Process Clause further protects a federal defendant's right to a jury trial by curtailing prosecutorial decisions that affect the racial composition of juries.[63] Nonetheless, in some cases, federal prosecutors have deliberately used Project Exile to secure a jury with a different racial composition than would otherwise be available at the state level. Project Safe Neighborhoods' mission to take Exile nationwide will only exacerbate that unseemly tactic.

In Richmond, Virginia, where Project Exile was first implemented, the jury pool for the state-level circuit court is approximately 75 percent African-American. In contrast, the jury pool for the Eastern District of Virginia, from which federal criminal juries are drawn in the Richmond area, is only about 10 percent African-American. Those facts were not lost on the federal prosecutors working on Project Exile cases in Richmond. At a Richmond Bench-Bar conference discussing Project Exile, a federal prosecutor stated that one of the program's goals was avoiding "Richmond juries." Another prosecutor made a similar admission at the sentencing hearing in *United States v. Scates*, a Project Exile case.[64]

In the 1999 case of *United States v. Jones*, a federal district court considered, and rejected, a Project Exile defendant's claim that such statements of bias revealed a prosecutorial design to affect the racial composition of his jury and thus violated his right to equal protection of the laws. Although the court expressed its "concern about the discretion afforded individuals who divert cases from state to federal court for prosecution under Project Exile," it was unwilling to hold that that discretion had been improperly exercised in this case, or that Project Exile had been systematically used to divert black defendants into the federal system and away from "Richmond juries." According to the court, the "desire to avoid Richmond juries" could be given "a less nefarious construction": "A 'Richmond jury' could simply be one bound by the laws of the Commonwealth of Virginia." The court invoked "the presumption of regularity afforded prosecutorial discretion" and refused to interpret the statements of the federal prosecutors as discriminatory.[65]

However, the court was disturbed by the lack of any discernible or judicially reviewable standards governing when a case should be assigned to federal rather than state court. It noted that Exile's design presented a real risk of selective federalization on the basis of race:

> If the process of diverting cases for federal prosecution is indeed independently accomplished by one unsupervised individual who is aware of the defendants' race, then Project Exile unnecessarily invites a substantial risk of selective prosecution. Indeed, if, as proponents of Project Exile maintain, there are disparities in the effectiveness of federal and state prosecutions then those disparities only increase the potential for discriminatory diversions for federal prosecution.[66]

Those risks are multiplied by Safe Neighborhoods' extension of the Exile model throughout all 50 states. Thus far, Safe Neighborhoods does not appear to include any standards to use in determining when it is appropriate to bring gun charges in federal, as opposed to state, court. That absence of standards for diverting cases to federal court, coupled with the close cooperation between federal and state officials that Safe Neighborhoods envisions, creates a real risk that prosecutors will divert cases that they perceive as racially charged to the federal system. Such forum-shopping tactics violate the guarantee of equal protection and undermine the constitutional right to a jury trial.

Are There Any Benefits? Is It Worth It?

The problems associated with the Bush administration's attempt to nationalize Project Exile under the auspices of Project Safe Neighborhoods have been noted. But what about the benefits? What do the American people get in exchange for weakening our federal structure and undermining our constitutional liberties?

Not much, as it turns out. Exile has been dramatically oversold by politicians and political activists who see in it a means of warding off restrictive gun control legislation. First of all, the legal tools available to state prosecutors pursuing armed felons are, in many cases, essentially the same as those available to federal prosecutors. Second, there is very little evidence that Exile has been the impetus for any dramatic reduction in crime in any city where it has been implemented.

In *United States v. Jones*, a panel of three federal judges examined Richmond's experience with Project Exile and concluded that Exile was superfluous, given that "the Commonwealth of Virginia possesses the same institutional mechanisms necessary to combat the problems Project Exile abdicates to federal prosecutors."[67] According to the court, the Virginia state statutes governing handgun crime are substantially similar to those at the federal level. Moreover, given its tough "three strikes" statute and its abolition of parole, Virginia law in some cases provides for harsher penalties for certain firearms offenses. Though rarely used in Virginia, the statutory provisions allowing the prosecutor to oppose pretrial release are also "substantively identical" to those available to federal prosecutors.[68]

In addition, the court found that Exile prisoners were not really "exiled" at all, despite U.S. Attorney Helen Fahey's claim that the prospect of serving time out of state was a major deterrent for criminals. As the court noted, "The vast majority of Project Exile defendants are incarcerated at the Northern Neck Regional Jail while awaiting trial and at the Federal Correction Institute in Petersburg, Virginia, following conviction."[69] Since the Virginia state penitentiary system has facilities located farther away from Richmond than either of those institutions, "Project Exile actually results in incarceration in facilities closer than many available in the state system." Accordingly, the court concluded that "the location of incarceration provides no justification for Project Exile."[70]

There is little evidence that Exile is the miracle cure its proponents claim. The homicide rate in Richmond fell 36 percent from 1997 to 1999, the period when Exile was most aggressively enforced.[71] But gun-related homicides and other violent crime dropped significantly all across the country during the same period, and criminologists do not agree about the cause of that decline.[72] For example, violent crime in New Orleans dropped 18 percent between 1997 and 1998, before it implemented an Exile program (Richmond's violent crime rate dropped by 19 percent during the same period).[73] Given the dearth of detailed research in the area, and the lack of a scholarly consensus on the causes of the nationwide decline in violent crime, a bit of humility about Project Exile's claims is in order.

Nonetheless, it stands to reason that if prosecutors make an aggressive effort to incarcerate armed felons—and if they focus on defendants who are likely to be future threats to society—such prosecutions can have an effect on the crime rate by getting a certain number of potential repeat offenders off the streets. But if a more aggressive crime control effort would bring substantial benefits, there is absolutely no reason that it cannot be undertaken by state law enforcement personnel. As the court in *United States v. Jones* put it, "While vigorous prosecution of firearms offenses has undoubtedly contributed to some unascertainable decline in the city's murder rate, there is no compelling reason to suspect that a comparable effort by local prosecutors would not achieve a comparable effect."[74]

Indeed, state legislatures are, all other things being equal, more responsive to local concerns than is the federal government. More important, state prosecutors are, for good or ill, generally more responsive to local pressure than are their federal counterparts. In most states, prosecutors are elected, whereas U.S. attorneys are presidential appointees. Thus, the states are likely to have greater incentive than the federal government to provide the level of protection that their citizens demand.

Even if Project Exile had the dramatic impact on crime that its most ardent supporters argue it does, its affront to the Constitution and the rule of law would compel constitutionalists to oppose it. But the available evidence suggests that its impact has been far more modest. Thus, the supporters of Project Exile and Project Safe Neighborhoods have failed to produce any compelling reason why systematic federal intervention is necessary. Given the costs federalization brings, that is a failure that should end the debate.

Federalism's Fair-Weather Friends

In the course of defending Project Exile, NRA executive director Wayne LaPierre Jr. attacked federal judges who have criticized the program: "They consider these nuisance cases, and the last thing federal judges want are armed felony cases in their courts. . . . That's shameful. Killing people is wrong, and . . . it needs to be changed. Every cop on the street knows it."[75] Although everyone can agree with LaPierre that "killing people is wrong," that obvious moral principle does not quite settle the debate over the federalization of crime. Something more is needed: a constitutional justification for nationalizing matters that have always been viewed as essentially local in nature. But no such justification has been forthcoming; NRA officials such as LaPierre and Charlton Heston repeatedly assailed President Bill Clinton for failing to enforce federal firearms statutes, without ever explaining why such cases should be in federal court. The supporters of federalizing gun crime lack even a compelling policy rationale—let alone constitutional grounds—for ignoring the distinction between local and interstate matters.

It is fairly clear that for supporters of the Second Amendment the main justification for federalizing gun crimes is political. Advocates of gun rights such as the NRA got behind the idea of nationalizing Project Exile because they made the judgment that a call to "enforce the gun laws on the books" could help ward off further gun control legislation. But even as a matter of political calculation, that may have been ill-considered. The strength of the gun control movement has been overestimated. For example, Al Gore's tough stance on guns was likely a net liability for him in the 2000 presidential election, costing him states such as West Virginia, Tennessee, and Arkansas. Al From of the centrist Democratic Leadership Council notes that 48 percent of voters in the 2000 election had guns in their households and many feared Democratic gun control proposals.[76] As Gore's running mate, Sen. Joe Lieberman (D-Conn.), described the ticket's experience with the gun issue, "We lost a number of voters who on almost every other issue realized they'd be better off with Al Gore."[77] And after September 11 support for gun control has eroded still further, according to a Gallup poll taken a month after the attacks.[78] "Any gun-control legislation of any kind is a non-starter now," says University of Virginia political scientist Larry Sabato.[79] Thus, the NRA's support for federalization initiatives seems to be a case in which political strategy has outlived the conditions that gave rise to it.

The "respect for federalism" President Bush and Attorney General Ashcroft publicly profess ought to find expression in their official conduct. There are disturbing indications, however, that it will not. As has been widely reported, where the administration disagrees with policies pursued by particular states, such as the legalization of assisted suicide and the use of medicinal marijuana, it has used the power of the federal government to intervene forcefully.[80] Project Safe Neighborhoods is of a piece with those actions, and no one who truly respects the Tenth Amendment and the doctrine of enumerated powers can support such an ill-conceived program.

Conclusion

In the wake of the September 11 terrorist attacks, some commentators have suggested that the constitutional principle of federalism is a luxury we can no longer afford.[81] But precisely the opposite is the case. The constitutional distinction between what is properly local and what is properly national has never been more important.[82] Combating the international threat of terrorism is a job for which the Constitution provides the federal government ample authority in the form of the power to declare war and to punish offenses against the laws of nations.[83] Prosecuting firearms offenses is a local issue, one that the Constitution properly leaves to states and localities. It is unwise to squander federal resources in the pursuit of offenders that the states and localities are perfectly equipped to handle. Even more important, we cannot afford to squander our constitutional heritage of limited government.

Project Safe Neighborhoods violates the constitutional principle of federalism. It also threatens to lead to overenforcement of gun laws and serious miscarriages of justice. If President Bush has the respect for federalism he professes, and if he takes seriously his oath to uphold the Constitution, he must drop Project Safe Neighborhoods.

Originally published as Cato Institute Policy Analysis no. 440, May 28, 2002.

Notes

1. "Remarks by the President at National Governors' Association Meeting," *U.S. Newswire*, February 26, 2001.
2. George Bush, "Remarks Announcing the Project Safe Neighborhoods Initiative in Philadelphia, Pennsylvania," *Public Papers of the Presidents*, May 21, 2001.
3. See "Sarah Brady Statement on White House Gun Safety Initiative," *U.S. Newswire*, May 14, 2001 ("Handgun Control has long supported strong enforcement of this nation's gun laws and tough prosecution programs like Project Exile"); "Schumer Lauds Project Exile Success in Rochester, Calls for National Expansion," Press release, office of Sen. Charles E. Schumer, March 30, 1999; and Tim Bryant, "Ashcroft Would Boost Efforts Here to Fight Illegal Guns," *St. Louis Post-Dispatch*, March 4, 2000, p. 8 ("Ashcroft said he favors implementation in St. Louis of the kind of anti-gun-crime effort authorities use in Richmond, VA [i.e., Project Exile]").
4. Toni Heinzl, "Richmond's Project Exile Criticized by Attorneys, Federal Judge," *Fort Worth Star-Telegram*, September 17, 2000, p. 21.
5. David Schiller, "Project Exile," www.vahv. org/Exile.
6. Helen F. Fahey, Testimony before the Senate Judiciary Committee, March 22, 1999. Copy in author's files.
7. Ibid.
8. Ibid.
9. See Michael Janofsky, "Attacking Crime by Making Federal Case of Gun Offenses," *New York Times*, February 10, 1999.
10. See David S. Cloud, "Prosecutor's Strategy Scrambles Gun-Control Alliances," *Wall Street Journal*, August 31, 1998.
11. See 18 U.S.C.A. § 922(g).
12. Fahey.
13. Elaine Shannon, "Have Gun? Will Travel," www.cnn.com/ALLPOLITICS/time/1999/08/09/gun.html.
14. Jim Abrams, "House OKs Bill Backing Gun Laws," *AP Online*, April 12, 2000.
15. R. H. Melton, "Bush Favors Va.-style Gun Control; Candidate Has National Hopes for Program Penalizing Felons," *Washington Post*, June 23, 1999.
16. "Project Safe Neighborhoods Fact Sheet," White House press release, May 14, 2001, www. whitehouse.gov/news/releases/2001/05/2001 0514-2.html. But note that in remarks given November 29, 2001, before the United States Attorneys Conference, President Bush stated that by September 2002, "we hope to have 200 new attorneys hired to prosecute crimes committed with a gun." *Public Papers of the Presidents*, December 3, 2001.
17. "Project Safe Neighborhoods Fact Sheet."
18. Bush.

19. See generally Adam H. Kurland, "First Principles of American Federalism and the Nature of Federal Criminal Jurisdiction," *Emory Law Journal* 45 (1996): 1.

20. Federalist Paper no. 45, in *The Federalist*, ed. George W. Carey and James McClellan (Dubuque, Iowa: Kendall-Hunt, 1990), p. 238.

21. Federalist Paper no. 17, in *The Federalist*, p. 85.

22. Thomas J. Maroney, "Fifty Years of Federalization of Criminal Law: Sounding the Alarm or 'Crying Wolf?' " *Syracuse Law Review* 50 (2000): 1319–20.

23. See Kathleen F. Brickey, "Criminal Mischief: The Federalization of American Criminal Law," *Hastings Law Journal* 46 (1995): 1139–40.

24. See generally, Roger Pilon, "Freedom, Responsibility, and the Constitution: On Recovering Our Founding Principles," *Notre Dame Law Review* 68 (1993): 507.

25. American Bar Association Task Force on the Federalization of Criminal Law, *The Federalization of Criminal Law*, 1998, p. 7.

26. Sara Sun Beale, "Legislating Federal Crime and Its Consequences: Federalizing Crime: Assessing the Impact on the Federal Courts," *Annals of the American Academy of Political and Social Science* 39 (January 1996): 43.

27. John S. Baker Jr., "State Police Powers and the Federalization of Local Crime," *Temple Law Review* 72 (1999): 683.

28. 18 U.S.C. § 2119; 8 U.S.C. § 1120; 18 U.S.C. § 247; and 18 U.S.C. § 43.

29. Given that the second plank in the Contract with America, the anti-crime Taking Back Our Streets Act, included federal aid to local law enforcement, there was also reason to be skeptical of the GOP's commitment to federalism. The Contract with America is available at www.house.gov/house/Contract/CONTRACT.html.

30. "We Will Continue in Our Drive to Return Power to Our States and Our People," *Washington Post*, January 5, 1995.

31. 514 U.S. 549 (1995).

32. Ibid., p. 567.

33. 521 U.S. 898 (1997).

34. 529 U.S. 598 (2000).

35. Pub. L. 107–110 (2002).

36. *Printz* at 921–22.

37. *United States v. Jones*, 36 F. Supp. 2d, 304, 316 (E.D. Va. 1999).

38. *United States v. Nathan*, 1998 U.S. Dist. LEXIS 15124 at *30 (E.D.Va. 1998).

39. John Ashcroft, "Gun Initiative/NICS," News conference, February 13, 2002, transcript, www.usdoj.gov/ag/speeches/2002/021302newsconference guninitiati-venics.htm. Federal prosecutions under Project Sentry will likely be conducted under 18 U.S.C.S. § 922(q), the revamped Gun-Free School Zones Act (Pub. L. 104–208, signed by President Clinton on September 30, 1996) enacted in the wake of *Lopez*. That act could be considered constitutional only under the narrowest possible reading of *Lopez*.

40. Jerry Seper, "Justice Takes Aim at Illegal Gun Possession," *Washington Times*, February 14, 2002.

41. *Lopez* at 564.

42. Thus far, Project Exile has proved itself largely immune to constitutional challenge in the federal courts. Despite the serious concerns about federalism expressed by the courts in *Jones, Nathan,* and other cases reviewing Exile's constitutionality, the federal judiciary has found itself constrained by existing precedents to uphold Exile. For example, although Exile uses state officers to enforce federal law, the jurisdictions participating in Exile programs are doing so voluntarily, not in response to a binding

federal mandate. Thus Exile does not fit precisely within the rule of *Printz v. United States*, the Brady Act case that held that the federal government could not forcibly "commandeer" state executive branch officials to enforce federal law. Similarly, the federal gun possession statutes on which the program principally relies have been upheld by various federal courts against *Lopez*-based challenges. See *United States v. Lewis*, 100 F.3d 49, 52 (7th Cir. 1996) ("A single journey across state lines, however remote from the defendant's possession, is enough to establish the constitutionally minimal tie of a given weapon to interstate commerce"); and *United States v. Pierson*, 139 F.3d 501, 504 (5th Cir. 1998) ("Evidence that a gun was manufactured in one state and possessed in another state is sufficient to establish a past connection between the firearm and interstate commerce"). It is difficult to see any reason—apart from judicial timidity—why that should be so. If, as *Lopez* held, Congress lacks the power under the Commerce Clause to proscribe carrying a gun within a school zone, it is hard to understand why the simple fact that a gun was manufactured out of state should be sufficient to proscribe intrastate possession of the weapon. If, as *Morrison* held, "the Constitution requires a distinction between what is truly national and what is truly local," and gender-motivated crimes of violence fall into the latter category, it is difficult to see why unlawful possession or use of a gun would fall in the former. Nonetheless, that is how the courts have come down. The Bush administration is no doubt counting on such case law to protect Safe Neighborhoods as well.

43. American Bar Association Task Force on the Federalization of Criminal Law, pp. 27–35.

44. Ibid., pp. 35–40.

45. Roberto Suro, "Rehnquist: Too Many Offenses Are Becoming Federal Crimes," *Washington Post*, January 1, 1999.

46. Tom Campbell, "Bull's Eye or Wasted Shots? Federal Judges Not among Gun Program's Supporters," *Richmond Times Dispatch*, January 22, 1999.

47. Beale, pp. 47–51.

48. Quoted in James Gordon Meek, "Is Federal Court Logjam on the Way?" *Lexis-ONE*, August 30, 2001.

49. See *South Dakota v. Dole*, 483 U.S. 203, 210 (1987) (holding that despite the Tenth Amendment, Congress can use spending power to encourage state-level legislative change by attaching conditions to receipt of federal grants).

50. *United States v. Morrison*, which struck down provisions of the Violence against Women Act, establishes the unconstitutionality of federal legislation criminalizing rape and sexual assault. But it doesn't stand in the way of federal funds to hire full-time state-level sex crime prosecutors.

51. See Dorothy Rabinowitz, "Only in Massachusetts," *Wall Street Journal*, December 29, 1999; and Dorothy Rabinowitz, "The Pursuit of Justice, Continued," *Wall Street Journal*, October 7, 1999.

52. Case law cannot be used to excuse the president's official actions. The president's duties as a constitutional official go beyond simply doing whatever the courts will let him get away with. As Justice Felix Frankfurter put it, "The ultimate touchstone of constitutionality is the Constitution itself and not what [the Court] has said about it." *Graves v. O'Keefe*, 306 U.S. 466, 491 (1938). The president has an independent duty arising from his oath of office to ensure that his powers are exercised pursuant to the Constitution.

53. To take one example of a garbage gun charge, a few years ago federal prosecutors charged Candisha Robinson with "using" a firearm during a drug offense. That

dubious charge arose out of the following circumstances. Undercover police officers made a controlled drug buy from Robinson at her apartment. The police later returned and executed a search warrant. Inside a locked trunk in the bedroom closet, the police found an unloaded handgun. Robinson received a 60-month term of imprisonment on that charge. See *Bailey v. United States*, 516 U.S. 137 (1995) (companion case). Although it is true that the conviction was ultimately overturned by the Supreme Court, the point here is to show the poor prosecutorial judgment in bringing that charge in the first place.

54. Quoted in Mark Fazlollah and Peter Nicholas, "U.S. Overstates Arrests in Terrorism," *Philadelphia Inquirer*, December 16, 2001.

55. See 18 U.S.C.A. § 922(d)(3), (6).

56. 18 U.S.C.A. § 922(g)(8)(c)(ii), prohibiting gun possession by anyone under a court order that "by its terms explicitly prohibits the use, attempted use, or threatened use of physical force against such intimate partner or child that would reasonably be expected to cause bodily injury"; See also *United States v. Emerson*, 46 F. Supp. 2d 598 (N.D. Tex. 1999); but see *United States v. Emerson*, 270 F.3d 203 (5th Cir. 2001) (suggesting that such a finding of fact is necessary in most states before a restraining order can be issued).

57. Quoted in Toni Heinzl, "Richmond's Project Exile Criticized by Attorneys, Federal Judge," *Fort Worth Star-Telegram*, September 17, 2000, p. 21.

58. David Holthouse, "Living in Exile: Federal Prisons Are Filling Up with People Whose Only Crime Is the Possession of a Gun," *Denver Westword*, March 21, 2002.

59. Quoted in ibid.

60. Tom Jackman, "Va. Jurists Denounce Mandatory Sentences; Felons with Guns Get No Breaks," *Washington Post*, October 9, 1999.

61. Gary Fields, "'Career Felons' Feel the Long Arm of Gun Laws," *Wall Street Journal*, July 3, 2001. For examples of the kinds of prosecutions that ideologically driven prosecutors might bring, see Guy Taylor, "Self-Defense Stance Defended on Web in Burglar Death," *Washington Times*, December 17, 2001, detailing the state-level prosecution, for first-degree murder and various gun charges, of two Maryland men who shot a burglar in self-defense. As the state's attorney prosecuting the case explained, "We have a comprehensive strategy in Baltimore for dealing with crimes with guns and reducing gun violence . . . the killing of Mr. Walker was not a typical street crime, but it is a crime that needs to be prosecuted." See also Tom Schoenberg, "Does Punishment Fit the Crime? He Turned In Gun, Now Faces Deportation," *Legal Times*, January 24, 2000, p. 1, describing the prosecution, by the District of Columbia U.S. Attorney's Office, of one Elwyn Lehman. Lehman, the driver of the tour bus for gospel singer CeCe Winans, brought the singer to the White House for a special tour. The 53-year-old driver had a handgun on board, but only realized this once he was at the gates of the White House. Lehman told the Secret Service officers about the pistol and voluntarily turned it over to them. He was rewarded with a trip to the D.C. Jail and charged with three counts of weapons possession. Lehman, a Canadian citizen who had been living in the United States for the past 15 years, also faced deportation. As the spokesman for the D.C. U.S. Attorney's Office explained, "Because the District of Columbia, which has one of the strictest gun laws in the country, continues to be plagued by an alarmingly high rate of gun violence, the U.S. attorney's office has long had a no-drop and zero-tolerance policy regarding persons found in illegal possession of firearms."

62. The incentives set up by Project Safe Neighborhoods may well place Safe Neighborhoods prosecutors in an uncomfortable ethical bind. In some cases, a prosecutor has an ethical obligation to decline to prosecute when circumstances warrant it. The A.B.A. standards state that "the prosecutor is not obliged to present all charges which the evidence might support." Among the factors that the prosecutor should consider in declining to prosecute are "the extent of the harm caused by the offense" and "the disproportion of the authorized punishment in relation to the particular offense or the offender." One wonders how an ambitious Safe Neighborhoods prosecutor will be able to fulfill this ethical obligation.

63. See *Batson v. Kentucky*, 476 U.S. 79 (1986).

64. *Jones* at 307–8 cites the sentencing transcript of *U.S. v. Scates*, 2001 U.S. App. LEXIS 10624, 11 Fed Appx 208 (4th Cir. 2001) to show that in at least one other Exile case a prosecutor admitted that one motivation for federalization was to get a different jury pool.

65. Ibid. Similar results were reached in *United States v. DeLoach*, No. 99-4441, 2000, U.S. App. LEXIS 3824 (4th Cir. 2000) and *United States v. Scates*.

66. *Jones* at 312.

67. Ibid. at 315.

68. Ibid. at 315; see also *United States v. Nathan*, 1998 U.S. Dist. LEXIS 15124 at *26.

69. *Jones* at 316.

70. Ibid.

71. See "Call in the Feds," *The Economist*, April 3, 1999.

72. Lorraine Adams and David A. Vise, "Crime Rates Down for 7th Straight Year; Experts Disagree about Reasons for Drop and the Meaning of Conflicting Trends," *Washington Post*, October 18, 1999.

73. Baker, p. 683.

74. *Jones* at 315.

75. Quoted in Janofsky.

76. Miles Benson, "Demos Drafting Own Contract with America; Party Leaders Want to Close 'Culture Gap,' " *New Orleans Times-Picayune*, July 18, 2001, p. 6.

77. Quoted in "DNC: Get Your Stinking Paws Off Gun Policy!" *The Hotline*, August 13, 2001.

78. Dante Chinni and Tim Vanderpool, "More in U.S. Carry Guns; Restrictions Lose Support," *Christian Science Monitor*, December 6, 2001.

79. Quoted in ibid.

80. See Nelson Lund, "Why Ashcroft Is Wrong on Assisted Suicide," *Commentary*, February 2002; and "U.S. Raid Sets Off Protests," *New York Times*, February 13, 2002.

81. See Linda Greenhouse, "Will the Court Reassert National Authority?" *New York Times*, September 30, 2001, suggesting that "the Supreme Court's federalism revolution has been overtaken by events."

82. See Marci Hamilton, "Federalism and September 11: Why the Tragedy Should Convince Congress to Concentrate Fully on Truly National Topics," *Findlaw Legal Commentary*, writ.news.findlaw.com/hamilton/20011025.html.

83. Though even here much of the responsibility for domestic safety will fall to states and localities. See Jonathan Walters, "Safety Is Still a Local Issue: This Is a Time for Every Level of Government to Remember the Things It Does Best," *Governing*, November 2000.

6. Misguided Guidelines: A Critique of Federal Sentencing

Erik Luna

November 1, 2002, marked the 15th anniversary of the U.S. Sentencing Guidelines. But there were no celebrations, parades, or other festivities in honor of the punishment scheme created by Congress and the U.S. Sentencing Commission. Instead, the day passed like most others during the intervening decade and a half—with scores of federal defendants sentenced under a convoluted, hypertechnical, and mechanical system that saps moral judgment from the process of punishment.

The Guidelines refer to the legal framework of rules for sentencing convicted federal offenders. After a defendant has been investigated by law enforcement, indicted by grand jury, and found guilty at trial (or through a plea bargain), the trial judge must determine an appropriate punishment under the Guidelines. Depending on the crime of conviction and various factors related to the offender and the offense, a federal judge will typically sentence the convicted defendant to a term of imprisonment and possibly a criminal fine. Of course, the federal system is dwarfed by the combined criminal justice systems of the individual states, the primary crime fighters in American society. Of the nearly 2 million inmates in the United States, fewer than 10 percent are presently serving federal sentences.[1]

Nonetheless, the federal system remains influential in the national debate on crime and punishment, presenting a prominent model for other jurisdictions in their penological experimentation. For better or worse, federal law enforcement continues to dominate certain categories of crime—such as drug offenses, immigration violations, and white-collar crime—often to the point of occupying the field. This tendency, particularly for narcotics offenses,[2] has only increased since the enactment of the Sentencing Guidelines, resulting in a federal prison population that has quadrupled in just a decade and a half.[3] In 1999, for example, more than 50,000 offenders were sentenced pursuant to the Guidelines, 44 percent of whom had been convicted of drug offenses.[4]

Some commentators have tried to distinguish the Guidelines from another federal sentencing phenomenon: mandatory minimum sentences.[5] But both the Guidelines and statutory minimums are manifestations of the same trend—mandatory or "determinate" sentencing. It is almost Orwellian doublespeak to call the present regime *guidelines*, given that judges must follow these sentencing rules or face reversal by appellate courts. In fact, the commission has even made the "Freudian slip"[6] of calling the Guidelines "mandatory."[7] Both mandatory minimums and the Guidelines attempt to purge sentencing discretion in federal trial courts, all but precluding judges from departing from the strictures of determinate punishment. Far from being alternatives, these two schemes feed off each other in curbing judicial discretion. For that reason, both the Sentencing Guidelines and mandatory minimums will be collectively referred to in this chapter as the "Guidelines."

Although the Guidelines are frowned upon from all corners of the criminal justice system, the federal judiciary has been particularly adamant in its opposition to the current sentencing regime. Federal judges have described the Guidelines as "a dismal failure," "a farce," and "out of whack;"[8] "a dark, sinister, and cynical crime management program" with "a certain Kafkaesque aura about it;"[9] and "the greatest travesty of justice in our legal system in this century."[10] In 1990, the Federal Courts Study Committee received testimony from 270 witnesses—including judges, prosecutors, defense attorneys, probation officers, and federal officials—and only four people expressed support for the Guidelines: the U.S. Attorney General and three members of the U.S. Sentencing Commission.[11] Surveys of the judiciary have confirmed widespread disapproval of the Guidelines: A 1997 survey concluded that more than two-thirds of federal judges view the Guidelines as unnecessary.[12]

With more than 15 years of overwhelmingly negative reaction, it is time to reconsider the Guidelines and their consequences for federal criminal justice.

Judge as Social Worker: Sentencing before the Guidelines

Like the proverbial road to hell, the path to the Guidelines was paved with good intentions. Federal sentencing was indeterminate in nature throughout much of the 20th century, allegedly pursuant to the rehabilitative ideal fostered by American prison reformers.[13] Primary control over sentencing was vested in the district court. With few exceptions, Congress provided only maximum terms of incarceration for federal crimes, allowing trial judges unbounded discretion to sentence offenders short of the upper limit—including no prison time at all (probation). Federal trial judges played a role that was part social worker, part soothsayer—gauging the length of sentence on the basis of an unguided evaluation of the necessary conditions for rehabilitation and indoctrination of pro-social behavior. To be sure, this regime suffered from several serious defects. Sentencing judges were dictatorial in practice: The district court was not required to provide reasons for any particular punishment, and so long as the term was within the broad statutory boundaries, the sentence was not subject to review on appeal. As a result, the federal system lacked any mechanism that might ensure a degree of inter-case equity in punishment.

Scholars and practitioners came to regard the system as fundamentally unfair and "lawless,"[14] spurring a somewhat remarkable confluence of critics, each with his own set of grievances. Civil rights activists contended that sentence length was often correlated with disturbing classifications, such as race and socioeconomic status. In contrast, political conservatives condemned the prevailing system for allowing "bleeding heart" judges to dole out lenient punishment for hardened criminals.[15]

Despite those differences, critics apparently agreed that largely unlimited judicial discretion, without written justifications and appellate review, tended to produce intolerable sentencing discrepancies between similarly situated offenders.[16] With some judges serving as well-intentioned social engineers and others as pseudoempirical shamans, punishment often depended on which courtroom door a defendant entered.

Judge as Accountant: Sentencing under the Guidelines

Although a few scholars have questioned the existence of capricious variations among truly comparable criminals,[17] the image and anecdotes of unequal punishment became widely accepted in the 1970s and early 1980s. Among others, Marvin Frankel was a particularly influential voice against the prevailing discretion in sentencing.

His 1973 book, *Criminal Sentences: Law without Order*, lambasted the federal system for its "unruliness, the absence of rational ordering, the unbridled power of the sentencers to be arbitrary and discriminatory,"[18] all of which should be "terrifying and intolerable for a society that professes devotion to the rule of law."[19] Judge Frankel's remedy was the establishment of an administrative agency—"a commission on sentencing"[20]—to develop rules that would provide direction for trial courts in determining appropriate punishment. The agency would be insulated from political pressures that distort rational decisionmaking, Frankel argued, and over time the administrators would develop a level of expertise beyond that of congressional generalists.

Behind Judge Frankel's proposal was an abiding conviction that the bureaucratic model of modern society could apply jot-for-jot to the practice of punishment. Sentencing could be pursuant to a "detailed profile or checklist of factors that would include, wherever possible, some form of numerical or other objective grading."[21] The resulting "chart or calculus" would be used "by the sentencing judge in weighing the many elements that go into a sentence."[22] Frankel even foresaw "the possibility of using computers as an aid toward orderly thought in sentencing."[23] He dreamed of a scientific jurisprudence that limited the discretion of judges through a systematic and all-encompassing body of rules, mechanically applying the law to a set of facts and thereby generating a proper sentence without the vagaries of trial-judge decisionmaking.

In practice, however, Judge Frankel's vision has proved to be more fantasy than reality. The Sentencing Commission has never been insulated from politics, and Frankel's mechanical sentencing regime subtracts precisely what is needed most in the human drama of punishment—moral judgment.

The Makeover: The Sentencing Reform Act Creates the Sentencing Commission

As legend would have it, the genesis of federal sentencing reform can be dated to a 1975 party hosted by Sen. Edward M. Kennedy (D-Mass.).[24] Among the invitees was Judge Frankel, whom Kennedy would later declare "the father of sentencing reform."[25] The dinner conversation with Frankel and other guests, including criminal justice scholar Alan Dershowitz, inspired the Massachusetts Democrat to lead the charge for a congressional overhaul of federal sentencing as it then existed. Although his initial bill was defeated, Senator Kennedy continued the campaign for sentencing reform, compromising here and there, and eventually garnering the support of an odd coalition of political luminaries including Sens. Joseph Biden (D-Del.), Orrin Hatch (R-Utah), and Strom Thurmond (R-S.C.).[26] Yet even with modifications to suit the needs of disparate interest groups, the Sentencing Reform Act barely passed as a rider to a general crime control bill.[27]

In classic congressional style, the act presented an extravagant set of legislative objectives and statutory requirements. Among its goals were to create a system that (1) promoted respect for the law; (2) offered a clear statement of the purposes of punishment as well as the available kinds and lengths of sentences; (3) ensured that the offender, federal officials, and the public "are certain about the sentence and the reasons for it"; (4) met the sometimes conflicting demands of retribution, deterrence, incapacitation, and rehabilitation; (5) provided trial judges with "a full range of sentencing options from which to select the most appropriate sentence in a particular case"; and (6) eliminated "unwarranted sentence disparities" between otherwise similarly situated criminals.[28]

The act ended indeterminate sentencing in the federal system, eliminating parole and requiring that judges set a specific term to be served in full (with a small allowance for good behavior) subject to appellate review. The act also established the U.S. Sentencing Commission—an "independent commission in the judicial branch"[29]—that was charged with promulgating guidelines that limited the punishment range to 25 percent of the maximum sentence.[30] These guidelines were supposed to capture pertinent aspects of the offender and the offense, and toward that end, Congress instructed the commission to "consider" the relevance of various factors surrounding the crime and the characteristics of the criminal, such as age, education, vocational skills, mental and emotional problems, physical condition, previous employment record, and family ties and responsibilities.[31]

By statute, the commission included two ex officio members and seven voting members, the latter composed of three sitting federal judges and no more than four individuals from the same party.[32] The enormous task facing the original commissioners was exacerbated by a deadline of a mere 18 months in which to formulate a whole new federal sentencing system. From the start, the original commission was mired in the confusing directives of the act and its legislative history, divided over the relevance and application of punishment philosophy, and dogged by critics who saw the entire enterprise as unconstitutional, unwise, or both. And, as will be discussed below, the eventual work product—the U.S. Sentencing Guidelines— showed all the scars of a political struggle within a poorly designed institutional process.

In theory, the Sentencing Guidelines delineate an appropriate sentence for each and every case through the application of detailed rules. Using these rules, the trial judge must first determine which of 43 categories governs the crime, thereby providing the "base offense level" for sentencing. The judge must next determine which of six "criminal history" categories applies to the defendant given his prior record of offending. With that information, the judge will then turn to the "Sentencing Table," a matrix of offense levels and criminal history scores that creates a 258-box grid of all potential punishment ranges for federal offenders. Grade the crime and the criminal record, find each on the grid, and where the axes meet, the applicable sentencing range will be found. The range might then be adjusted by aggravating circumstances, such as the defendant's brandishing of a weapon, or mitigating circumstances, such as the defendant's accepting responsibility for his criminal misconduct.

The Supreme Court Sanctions the Unconstitutional Commission

The commission and its Guidelines suffer from a number of shortcomings that justify a sweeping reconsideration of the current federal system. The first and arguably dispositive problem is the delegation of lawmaking authority—specifically, the power to set punishment—from Congress to the commission. Despite dubious constitutionality, the commission and its Guidelines were upheld by the U.S. Supreme Court in *Mistretta v. United States* (1989).[33] In a scathing dissent, Justice Antonin Scalia described the commission as "a sort of junior-varsity Congress,"[34] effectively empowered to make law by prescribing the punishment for criminal defendants. Among other things, this "new Branch"[35] of government sets the range of punishment, defines when probation is permissible, regulates whether criminal fines should be levied and in what amounts, and determines those characteristics of offenses and offenders that are relevant in sentencing. As Justice Scalia noted, such decisions are not technical or procedural, but are instead substantive value and policy judgments that the Constitution has vested in the political branches.[36] As a matter of constitutional text and structure, "all legislative Power ... shall be vested"[37] in Congress, meaning that only the national legislative body can create federal law. Yet under the Sentencing Reform Act, the commission's dictates become law—binding on individual parties and the federal courts—absent presidentially approved congressional legislation to the contrary.[38]

Moreover, the creation of the commission and its Guidelines has blurred the line of accountability for any particular sentence and for punishment policy in general. Congress concocted an administrative agency that is supposedly lodged in the judicial branch, whose members are chosen by the president and approved by Congress to serve a specified term. But unlike other agencies, the commission is largely freed from statutory constraints typically placed on administrative bodies, including regularized procedures for considering new rules, a commitment to open meetings and discussions, detailed explanations for the issuance of new rules, and review by the courts under an "arbitrary and capricious" standard.[39] As a result, the commission can act without defending its decisions or its decisionmaking process. The sentences for violent crimes were increased, for instance, "where the Commission was convinced that they were inadequate"[40]—without any explanation as to what made a punishment "inadequate" or how the commissioners became "convinced" that this was the case for a particular offense.

Despite the fact that its composition and activities often seem to have a partisan attachment, the commission lacks a direct line of accountability to any of the three branches and remains largely anonymous to the general public. The Supreme Court's "nonpolitical" label to the contrary,[41] the commission was a politicized entity from the beginning, composed of party adherents and aspirants to higher office, but lacking any members with significant experience in the practice of sentencing.[42] At least under the prior, thoroughly political regime, the citizenry knew whom to blame for any grievances with federal punishment—Congress for enacting the relevant legislation and the president for signing it into law. But with the commission and its Guidelines, no politically accountable entity can be held responsible for the failures of federal sentencing law.

Shift in Power Spawns a "Prosecutor's Paradise"

The Guidelines and the commission rest upon a dubious constitutional foundation, but the regime suffers from other problems as well, most notably the dehumanization of the punishment process and the elimination of legitimate judicial discretion. The absence of moral judgment under the Guidelines stems at least in part from a radical change within the power structure of federal criminal justice, with the Sentencing Reform Act drastically shifting the traditional balance between legislative and judicial branches. Throughout most of American history, lawmakers broadly defined criminal offenses and potential punishments while judges determined the comparative seriousness of a specific crime and an appropriate sentence for the offender. As noted earlier, some commentators and practitioners expressed grave concerns about the unbounded discretion of federal trial judges in the indeterminate sentencing era. But that situation has now been reversed: The current system of punishment has wrested from the district court almost all power to determine the relevance and weight of various factors or characteristics concerning the offense and offender, as well as limiting the range of potential sentences and the court's authority to depart from the Guidelines.

If the shift in power were only from judges to lawmakers, a main concern would be the political distortion of sentencing in federal courts. Because "tough on crime" platforms tend to have electoral appeal, legislators often play to voters' short-term emotions rather than considering sound public policy, producing criminal justice initiatives with few real benefits to society but large financial and human costs. Some national lawmakers thought the act would avoid the politicization of punishment by shifting sentencing power from the courts to the commission, rather than to Congress itself. But a number of scholars have shown that the commission simply became another political body, influenced by interest groups and susceptible to many of the pressures placed on lawmakers.[43] One former commissioner recently claimed, for instance, that gratuitous increases in punishment for robbery and fraud were propelled by political heat from the Department of Justice.[44]

In one sense, the commission is *worse* than a political body, issuing a set of "diktats"[45] that command specific consequences in sentencing while remaining unaccountable for any disastrous results. In modern constitutional democracies, sentencing rules are deemed legitimate because they are the product of politically accountable processes and warranted by logic or empirical evidence. As suggested earlier, neither condition holds true for the unaccountable commission and its unjustified Guidelines. Moreover, the commission may have usurped more power for itself than even Congress had originally anticipated. For example, the Guidelines and subsequent interpretations by the commission frequently prohibit trial judges from considering facts about the offender that may be highly relevant in fixing an appropriate punishment. Yet the decision to preclude at sentencing any consideration of the defendant's age, employment history, family responsibilities, and so on, was not expressly ordered by lawmakers, nor even implicitly suggested by the congressional record. Instead, the commission made those and other decisions of its own accord and without a clear legislative mandate.

To be sure, Congress and the commission maintain a symbiotic relationship in the control of federal sentencing. Lawmakers send the commission "directives" for new guidelines or sentencing factors, which the commission invariably "considers" and adopts.[46] Congress has also enacted the aforementioned mandatory minimums, which necessarily influence the Sentencing Guidelines and the permissible range of punishment for relevant crimes. In turn, the commission's work product becomes law unless reversed by congressional legislation to the contrary. But for present purposes, whether the sentencing buck stops with lawmakers or commissioners is beside the point. To the extent that a criminal sentence is preordained by Congress or the commission, individuals are being judged by a distant body that lacks any meaningful understanding of the offense or the offender. Without firsthand knowledge of the case at bar, these far-off entities can only supply cookie-cutter justice that rests on generalities rather than a moral judgment framed by experience and the holistic assessment of a real human being.

What neither Congress nor the commission may have expected, however, was that the abatement of judicial discretion in sentencing would greatly amplify the authority of federal prosecutors. Limiting the power of judges at the final stage of criminal justice necessarily expands the decisionmaking authority of prosecutors at early points in the process. In fact, the Guidelines have proven to be "a prosecutor's paradise,"[47] at least for those prosecutors who crave control over sentencing. To begin with, federal prosecutors exercise greater

127

power than ever through their charging and plea-bargaining decisions. The Guidelines not only threaten severe punishment but also hem in judges through tight sentencing ranges and limited means of departure from those parameters. As a result, defendants often face substantial prison time without the possibility of judicial leniency.

In Professor Albert Alschuler's metaphor, the Guidelines serve as the classic "bad cop," intimidating the accused defendant with the possibility of a long prison sentence.[48] Federal prosecutors can then play the part of "good cop" by offering a deal that the defendant literally cannot refuse—unless, of course, he or she is willing to risk a lengthy prison term by standing trial.

Government leverage in plea bargaining is further enhanced by the prosecutor's unique power to facilitate deviations from the Guidelines. Although judges have few grounds to depart from a given sentencing range, prosecutors have the exclusive and unreviewable authority to seek a "downward departure" based on "substantial assistance" from the defendant. Because the Guidelines often tie the hands of judges at sentencing, the prosecutor's unilateral authority over "substantial assistance" departures provides yet more government leverage over the defendant and his constitutional rights.

For a concrete example, consider the bust of a small drug ring in northern Virginia.[49] Through weeks of surveillance, federal law enforcement personnel documented sales totaling more than 50 grams of crack cocaine, the minimum amount needed to trigger a mandatory 10-year sentence for every individual associated with the drug ring. More than a dozen suspects were arrested, most of whom were in their early 20s, and their convictions were all but preordained in federal district court. The punishment each defendant received, however, was not a function of whether he was a major participant in the ring or just a bit player. Instead, those who cooperated with federal prosecutors by turning in their friends secured lower sentences through "substantial assistance" departures. The drug ring's lieutenant and two major dealers admitted their active involvement in distributing crack cocaine, sold out their colleagues, and in return received sentences of five years or less. In contrast, three minor dealers (two of whom were teenagers at the time) refused to cooperate with prosecutors and were sentenced to

12 years in federal prison. As the U.S. Attorney admitted, cooperating with law enforcement was "the only ticket to freedom."[50] Although such cooperation has always been a factor at sentencing, federal prosecutors in the executive branch, rather than impartial judges, now determine who is eligible for leniency.

Prosecutors also exert vast power through the Guidelines' "real offense" scheme, which requires judges to sentence defendants on the basis of "relevant conduct" presented by the government. This conduct includes any acts related to the crime of conviction, including all reasonably foreseeable behavior and even those acts that were not part of the underlying crime but were connected to "the same course of conduct or common scheme or plan."[51] Such conduct need only be proven by a preponderance of the evidence, may be based on hearsay, and can include acts for which the defendant was acquitted.[52]

Consider Vernon Watts, who was arrested after police detectives found cocaine in his kitchen cabinet and loaded guns in his bedroom closet.[53] At trial, the jury convicted Watts on the drug charges but acquitted him of "using a firearm" during a narcotics-related crime. Despite an acquittal on the weapons charge, the sentencing court announced that Watts indeed possessed the guns in connection with the drug offense and that his sentence would be increased accordingly. As bizarre as it may sound, Watts will serve additional time in prison for the acquitted conduct.

In addition, the Guidelines give prosecutors an incentive to reserve important facts or serious charges until sentencing to take advantage of looser evidentiary rules. In one case, the government prosecuted a man for robbery but waited until the sentencing phase to tell the court that he was also a murderer.[54] In another case, prosecutors dropped a weapons charge at trial but then reintroduced the matter as relevant conduct at the sentencing phase to significantly enhance an individual's prison term.[55] More frequently, the government provides postconviction evidence that drastically increases, for instance, the amount of drugs attributable to the defendant, thereby generating a sentence many times greater than what was possible under the original charge.[56]

In *United States v. Rodriguez*,[57] the defendant was prosecuted for various drug offenses related to his delivery of 10 ounces of marijuana. The jury struggled over the issue of guilt, convicting the defendant of a single count of conspiracy only after the judge pressured the jurors to reach a verdict.[58] On the basis of only the evidence produced at trial, the defendant should have received a prison term of 18–24 months. But after the jury was dismissed, prosecutors told the judge that the defendant had actually sold more than 1,000 kilos of marijuana. Using the lower, preponderance standard of proof, the trial court accepted the government's claims and sentenced the defendant to *life in prison without the possibility of parole*. Although affirmed on appeal, the decision was severely criticized by dissenting Judge Richard Posner:

> There is a serious question whether it is permissible to sentence a person to life in prison, without possibility of parole, at the end of a brief and casual sentencing hearing in which there is no jury, in which the rules of evidence are not enforced, in which the standard of proof is no higher than in an ordinary civil case, and in which the judge's decision will make the difference between a light punishment and a punishment that is the maximum that our system allows short of death.[59]

According to the majority ruling, however, Rodriguez received all the process he was due under the Guidelines. He will be in prison for life despite the jury's equivocation on his guilt and the diluted rules of evidence at his sentencing hearing.

The Absence of Moral Judgment

The overt transfer of sentencing authority from the judiciary to Congress and the commission, as well as the shift of power from trial judges to prosecutors, has undermined punishment as the product of moral judgment. Such decisionmaking requires an assessment of an individual as a human being by an entity capable of comprehending all that makes that individual unique. Obviously, moral judgment involves questions of abstract and universal justice, the rights and obligations that correspond to membership in a just society. But it is more than an academic inquiry; the necessary judgment requires sensitivity to complex questions raised by the exigencies of real life, where no single heuristic or guiding principle can guarantee an appropriate outcome. If a particular incident or course of conduct is at issue, the entity passing judgment must fully grasp what the events were, how they came to transpire, and what their ultimate effects on other persons or groups may be.

Making a moral judgment about an individual involved in a given incident also demands an understanding of the bigger picture that constitutes a person's life. Where did that individual come from? What are his personal attributes, good and bad? How does he treat others? Those questions and many more help to develop a three-dimensional human being with a past, present, and future, rather than a black-and-white caricature lacking depth and detail. An individual's capacity to do good and bad, to feel empathy and remorse, to acknowledge misdeeds and make amends, and so on, cannot be separated into discrete units, placed on a scale, and measured in inches or pounds. No numerical value can be assigned to each part that makes up an individual and plugged into an equation one at a time to spit out a bottom line. A person can only be judged as a whole, with the entirety of his life placed in the metaphysical balance, measured by an entity capable of making this type of context-sensitive, holistic assessment.

Distant government bodies such as Congress and the commission lack the capacity to evaluate the facts of a specific crime or the circumstances of a particular offender. They can only create classes of crimes and criminals that privilege certain factors and ignore others, transforming unique cases into uniform patterns more agreeable to conveyor-belt treatment. A far-off agency can no more judge specific criminals than a blindfolded expert can appraise the worth of unseen paintings. It is true, of course, that prosecutors are privy to the evidence and present for the proceedings, but let's be clear—government prosecutors are partisans in the criminal justice system. Although charged to "do justice," they often seem preoccupied with obtaining guilty verdicts in an occupation in which job performance is typically evaluated by "conviction rate." That is not a slight against government attorneys but is perhaps an unavoidable consequence of the prevailing "battle model" of criminal litigation.[60] Sometimes, the adversarial nature of their position prevents prosecutors from neutrally evaluating the evidence and assessing the defendant as an individual, rather than as a means to an end.

Only a trial court—learned in the law, guided by experience, and dispassionate in decisionmaking—can morally judge a convicted criminal. The personal assessment of facts and circumstances, along with the interaction between judge and defendant, provides the basis for a court's imposition of moral judgment in the form of a sentence. This weighing of often disparate and incommensurable factors cannot be done by algorithm or from afar.

Unfortunately, this type of moral judgment is largely precluded by the Guidelines. For instance, the "real offense" approach allows the court to factor in only aggravating behavior, provides no judicial discretion to temper the ultimate effect of such conduct on sentencing, and rejects other moral considerations such as previous acquittals. More generally, the punishment scheme promulgated by the commission and the aforementioned shift in discretion away from the courts have reduced the authority and legitimacy of federal sentencing.

The Inscrutable Guidelines

The Guidelines subvert moral judgment in three interrelated ways. First, the current system is confusing or downright incomprehensible to practitioners and lay citizens alike, while the hypertechnical nature of sentencing variations is hard to justify and only adds to the chaos. The Guidelines "seem to sacrifice comprehensibility and common sense on the altar of pseudo-scientific uniformity," Professor Kate Stith and Judge José Cabranes write in their book, *Fear of Judging*. The result has been sentencing hearings "nearly unintelligible to victims, defendants, and observers, and even to the very lawyers and judges involved in the proceeding."[61] The sentencing rules are contained in the *Guidelines Manual*, a document that has swelled over the past 15 years to more than 1,000 pages of complex regulations variously described as "Guidelines," "Policy Statements," and "Commentary," and filled with amendments, cross-references, and examples.

As might be expected, there is a serious shortage of practitioners who truly understand sentencing under the Guidelines. This general illiteracy—effected by the labyrinthine quality of federal punishment and compounded by hundreds of amendments and thousands of court cases—has inspired a cottage industry that, in turn, produces reams of publications intended to educate practitioners about the Guidelines. The commission and others have even set up telephone hot lines to steer attorneys and probation officers through the bewildering rules of federal sentencing.[62] But despite government and commercial assistance, the sheer complexity of the system ensures a high error rate in tallying federal sentences. The cases are legion of officials miscalculating sentence length, judges using wrong editions of the *Guidelines Manual*, attorneys failing to pick up computation errors, and so on, sometimes resulting in sentences that are off by years.[63]

Even when punishment is mathematically accurate, the Guidelines frequently recognize subtle differences that have little, if any, cognitive value, yet result in significant disparities in sentence length. Lines are drawn between "minor" and "minimal" participation in a crime, for instance, and between "leadership" and "managerial" roles in the offense. As former commissioner, now justice, Stephen Breyer said in 1998, "Ranking offenders through the use of fine distinctions is like ranking colleges or the 'liveableness' of cities with numerical scores that reach ten places past a decimal point. The precision is false."[64]

Unfortunately, neither the language of sentencing nor the Guidelines' visual aid, the "Sentencing Table," conveys to the common citizen the process and basis for punishment as a moral judgment. The federal criminal justice system now uses terms like "base levels," "categories," "points," "scores," and other jargon that sound more like a parlor game than the process for imposing sentence on real human beings. The Sentencing Table offers little help, with its complex matrix of offense levels and criminal history scores producing a 258-box grid that only an economist could love. Even an average person who comprehends the workings of the grid might still be left wondering what makes a level-10 crime worse than a level-9 crime, for instance, or why a level-15 crime receives about twice the sentence of a level-10 crime.

The excessive complexity of the Guidelines impedes understanding of the federal system in general and a given sentence in particular, transforming a human event into a string of terms and numbers. Consider the following sentencing colloquy reported by the *Washington Post*:

> The court finds that the base offense level is 20. . . . Pursuant to Guideline 2K2.1(B)(4), the offense level is increased by two levels [to 22]. . . . The court notes that the criminal convictions . . . result in a total criminal history category score of 18. At the time of the instant offense . . . the defendant was

> serving a parole sentence in two causes of action. And pursu-
> ant to Sentencing Guidelines 4A1.1(D), 2 points are therefore
> added. The total criminal history points is 20. And according
> to the sentencing guidelines Chapter 5, Part A, 20 criminal
> history points establish a criminal history category of 6. . . .
> [As a result] the guideline range for imprisonment is 84 to
> 105 months.[65]

Although the Sentencing Reform Act was supposed to provide
"certainty about the sentence and the reasons for it," the theoretical
and practical complexity of the Guidelines all but ensures that the
defendant and the general public will remain in the dark. Without
expert assistance, average citizens have no way of understanding
the body of federal crimes and their respective penalties.

The Mechanical Nature of the Guidelines

Federal sentencing has purged much of the human element necessary for moral judgment—a point that has not been lost on the
judiciary. One district court judge argued that "human conduct just
doesn't fit into a grid,"[66] while another judge assailed the Guidelines
as a "wholly mechanical sentence computation which desensitizes
those associated with it, and converts a sentencing proceeding, which
might otherwise have some salutary effect on the offender, to a
mathematical and logistical exercise."[67]

In many cases, the Guideline ranges are too narrow to adequately
fit the variations among crimes and criminals. Because a sentence
must be within 25 percent of the maximum, judges are left with
little room to accommodate either mitigating or aggravating circumstances not already factored into the equation. Sometimes the Guidelines set even tighter ranges than are required by statute. Consider,
for instance, a first-time offender convicted of an (otherwise) unre-
markable assault with a deadly weapon. In Utah, this defendant
could receive probation or serve up to five years in prison consistent
with the state's indeterminate sentencing procedures.[68] Under California's determinate scheme, the offender could be sentenced to as
little as six months in a local jail or as much as four years in the
state prison.[69] Using federal statutes *in the absence of the Guidelines*,
assault with a deadly weapon would result in a sentence of anywhere
from probation to 10 years of imprisonment.[70] But under the Guidelines, this aggravated assault calls for a sentence of 27 to 33

months[71]—a mere six-month range (or 18 percent of the maximum) within which the judge must tailor a fair resolution. That tight spread seems only marginally preferable to the commission setting an exact sentence itself.[72]

The most troubling restrictions, however, involve the use of relevant information and characteristics of the offender. "Traditionally," noted the Supreme Court in 1993, "sentencing judges have considered a wide variety of factors in addition to evidence bearing on guilt in determining what sentence to impose on a convicted defendant."[73] These factors included any information that might explain the defendant's behavior, provide insight into his potential for reform, or indicate significant effects on other parties as a consequence of the sentencing decision. By statute, the Guidelines were required to be "neutral" toward the offender's race, sex, national origin, and creed—a limitation that comports with American conceptions of equality and the major impetus for federal sentencing reform.[74] But the commission has barred an array of seemingly relevant factors from being considered by trial courts, including the following:

- age
- education
- vocational skills
- mental and emotional condition
- physical condition
- drug or alcohol dependence
- lack of guidance as a youth
- employment history
- family ties and responsibilities
- community ties
- military or public service
- charitable works[75]

In the past, judges would have considered most if not all of those factors during sentencing. A young person who went astray without parental support, for example, but who possesses an education and employable skills, might deserve mercy based on our natural empathy for wayward youth and the offender's potential for reform and eventual success in society. Likewise, a trial court might reduce a sentence because of the defendant's good employment record, strong ties to the community, responsibilities for underage dependents, and a history of philanthropic contributions. In such a case, the defendant has built up a reserve of goodwill that won't necessarily be annulled by his crime, while his record of employment and ties to family and community might suggest a high probability of reform and successful reintegration into society. Such factors could point in the other direction as well—for instance, a defendant with a poor educational and employment record despite strong adult guidance—possibly pushing the judge toward a longer sentence. Nonetheless, the Guidelines remove these morally relevant factors from the sentencing process.

To be clear, the current federal regime may make sense for the hypothetical "average defendant"—for example, a person ordinary in all respects, without a criminal history and individual traits that might aggravate or mitigate the sentence, who commits a generic assault with a firearm. A Guidelines sentence of 27–33 months might seem perfectly appropriate for this undistinguished offender and common crime. Consistent with the goals of sentencing reform, this range of punishment prevents judges from imposing an oppressive 10-year term of imprisonment or, conversely, a mere slap of probation. But the Guidelines' range may become unjust when human factors are added to the hypothetical, converting this mythical average defendant into a real and unique person. The young man with a strong record of education and employment, stable ties to family and community, a wife and children, and a history of volunteerism— who brandished a weapon in a one-time, nonlethal street altercation—must serve between two and three years in federal prison. In contrast, an older criminal with a spotty employment record, little education, and no vocational skills, who lacks ties to family and community and has a history of being a drug abuser, deadbeat dad, grifter, and drifter, will serve no more than 33 months of imprisonment regardless of an ignominious past and limited chance of personal transformation.

Of course, the Guidelines were supposed to end inconsistent treatment of offenders, a worthy cause by all appearances. But as Albert Alschuler has quipped, "Some things are worse than sentencing disparity, and we have found them."[76] Whatever its effects on *disparity*, the current federal regime has produced excessive *uniformity* in punishment, with significantly different offenders and offenses receiving similar sentences.

136

This problem has been recognized and criticized not only by members of the judiciary and academic opponents of the Guidelines, such as Alschuler and Michael Tonry,[77] but also by those who (cautiously) support the Guidelines regime, such as Stephen Schulhofer.[78] By privileging certain facts, particularly quantifiable details such as monetary loss or drug quantity, while ignoring morally relevant factors about the offender and his life, federal sentencing creates the *illusion* of eliminating unwarranted disparities. Though the Guidelines ensure that those who steal the same amount of money or sell the same quantity of drugs receive similar sentences, this "aggregation" of defendants in no way guarantees *equality*—the like treatment of similarly situated offenders who commit comparable crimes. As one former commissioner admitted, "The emphasis was more on making sentences alike, and less on ensuring the likeness of those grouped together for similar treatment."[79]

Consider Judge Pierre Leval's hypothetical of two offenders who independently embezzle $10,000 from a bank.[80] They may receive the same sentence even if one defendant is "universally known by coworkers, family and friends as honest, hard-working, loving and generous," and stole the money "to buy expensive medications that might save her child"—while the other defendant lived "a life of abused and wasted privilege," "cheated and deceived at every opportunity, [and] abandoned his first wife and children after exhausting his wife's money."[81] In such circumstances, it is difficult to argue that justice is done by doling out the same punishment to both defendants.

A comprehensive understanding of equality is also challenged by comparing the sentences for different crimes. Whereas second-degree murder is a base level-33 offense under the Guidelines, possessing 150 grams of crack cocaine with intent to sell is a level-34 offense. Given the large disparity of injury caused by these two crimes, it seems hard to fathom a moral system of sentencing that deems a drug offender similar to, let alone worse than, a murderer.[82]

An Open Secret: Routine Circumvention and Nullification of the Guidelines

A third and largely unreported problem with federal sentencing involves the hidden nullification of the Guidelines by criminal justice actors. In light of the problems discussed earlier, it is little wonder that some judges, prosecutors, and defense attorneys have circumvented the Guidelines' strictures to achieve a just outcome in individual cases. "There's a certain fiction we all engage in if we want a certain result," one defense attorney acknowledged.[83] Trial judges bothered by a particularly onerous punishment under the Guidelines, but unwilling to overtly disregard the rules, simply manipulate the actual facts of a case to reduce sentence calculations. Some judges have even instructed probation officers to tailor their reports (e.g., omit certain items) so as to be consistent with a preordained outcome.[84]

Federal prosecutors and defense attorneys also engage in their own machinations to evade the Guidelines through the use of clandestine agreements on those facts to be presented in open court. This process of "fact bargaining" results in counsel lying to the judge about, for instance, the amount of drugs or monetary loss, the dates of crime, or the existence of a firearm—all with the goal of skirting the federal rules and securing a lower sentence for the defendant.[85] As one probation officer notes, "The widespread use of fact bargaining, and the lying to the court that is inevitable with the frequent use of such bargaining, is the dirty little secret in the prosecution of federal criminal cases."[86] In a 1996 survey, less than one-fifth of probation officers reported that Guidelines calculations were factually accurate in most of the cases they had seen, while two-fifths of the respondents reported that calculations were more likely than not to be incorrect.[87] Moreover, Professor Schulhofer and former commissioner Ilene Nagel have found that the Guidelines are circumvented in at least 20–35 percent of all cases resolved by guilty plea.[88]

A recent appellate ruling detailed the plight of six defendants, all charged with conspiracy to distribute approximately 5,000 grams of crack cocaine over a 36-week period. Those who refused to cooperate with prosecutors were liable for the full quantity of drugs, resulting in punishment of around 20 years in prison. In contrast, the defendants who played ball with the government were held accountable for only a fraction of the crack cocaine and therefore received sentences of 5 years or less.[89] On appeal, the reviewing court admitted that the disparity caused by fact bargaining "would strike many as unfair" and "exacts a high price from those who exercise their constitutional rights to trial," although it concluded that the resulting inequity was of no constitutional moment.[90] A subsequent district court opinion, however, criticized the appellate decision as representing "a sad epiphany":[91]

> If fact bargaining is acceptable, then the entire moral and intellectual basis for the Sentencing Guidelines is rendered essentially meaningless. If "facts" don't really matter, neither does "judging" contribute anything to a just sentence. . . . "Facts are like flint," judges say, and their proper ascertainment is the crowning goal of our entire adversary system. When parties can "make up" their own facts with little fear of discovery and no effective sanction, however, courts no longer adjudicate actual cases and controversies, as required by the Constitution. They simply ratify the government's secret bargains with defendants, thus lending (and dissipating) their moral authority as an independent third branch of government.[92]

Fact bargaining is corrosive to the pursuit of truth, literally turning the world of criminal justice upside down. It is as though the Queen of Hearts had designed the whole process—sentence first, facts later—with the parties negotiating punishment and then working backward to a fact pattern supporting the outcome. Despite intentions to the contrary, the rigidity and excesses of the Guidelines have only encouraged dishonesty in service of other goals, with a wink and a nod between litigants and the court. "That's what makes it a sham," one defense attorney scoffed.[93]

But these sentencing shenanigans are more than a sham—they conflict with the idea of an open, representative democracy. Guidelines circumvention is "hidden and unsystematic," Schulhofer and Nagel suggest, occurring "in a context that precludes oversight and obscures accountability."[94] As a general rule, representative democracy requires accessibility of elected officials to the people, responsiveness of officials to popular demands, and accountability of officials for their decisions. In turn, accessibility, responsiveness, and accountability require honesty and some minimal amount of openness or transparency by the state. Without knowledge of the factual basis for official decisions, the public is unable to evaluate these judgments and therefore denied the opportunity to demand an accounting of the official's deeds and reasons.

If the nominal facts underlying Guideline sentences are different from the actual facts of the relevant cases, can the public correctly evaluate the effectiveness of federal law enforcement, for instance, or assess the law-and-order claims made by a local member of Congress? The answer must be "no" if accountability is predicated on truthful information rather than fabrications. In the words of one disgruntled district court judge: "The Guidelines . . . have made charlatans and dissemblers of us all. We spend our time plotting and scheming, bending and twisting, distorting and ignoring the law in an effort to achieve a just result. All under the banner of 'truth in sentencing'!"[95] The dishonesty spawned by the current regime may lead to cynicism and contempt of the Guidelines not only among practitioners and jurists, but also by the citizenry as it evaluates the legitimacy and trustworthiness of government, and thus the basis for general compliance with the law.[96]

Ironically, the Guidelines' crusade to eliminate disparities in sentencing may have only exacerbated the problem. Experience has shown that the federal scheme has not prevented sentencing discretion but has merely driven it underground to the hidden realm of legal contortions and fact bargaining. Whatever the shortcomings of the prior regime, at least sentencing determinations and any resulting disparities were made in the open. Now, much of the decisionmaking takes place behind closed doors, with collusion among the parties and even the judge to circumvent the Guidelines, subject to none of the disinfectant that sunlight provides.[97] The disparities in sentencing continue, with punishment depending on the location of the crime, the temperament of the prosecutor, the competence of defense counsel, and the craftiness of the judge.[98] The Guidelines have thus created the worst of all worlds: a formal system that prevents the court from considering a defendant's humanity combined with an underground process that secretly attempts to ameliorate the system's many failures.

The Perverse and Unjust Consequences

To be clear, many of the defendants serving time under the Guidelines are violent or serious criminals. The defendant in the aforementioned *Rodriguez* case, for instance, will never be a candidate for sainthood.[99] He had previously been convicted of possessing heroin and methaqualone, both with intent to distribute. In his latest conviction, the defendant allegedly transported hundreds of pounds of

140

marijuana from Texas to Wisconsin. As such, *Rodriguez* is a case unlikely to inspire empathy for the defendant and public outrage against the Guidelines. Yet under the American system of law, even brazen criminals charged with the most serious offenses are entitled to the full panoply of procedural protections guaranteed by the Constitution. The very integrity of the process is measured not by the rights accorded sympathetic defendants, but by the treatment provided the worst offenders in the criminal justice system. If it is unfair to sentence the most pitiful defendant to an elongated term on the basis of, for instance, evidence not presented to the jury and not found to be true beyond a reasonable doubt, it must also be deemed unjust to do the same thing to an unmitigated scoundrel.

More important, the practical injustices produced by the Guidelines have not been limited to the procedural claims of rogues and villains. There are countless horror stories of low-level or minor offenders, with compelling arguments in mitigation of their crimes, who nonetheless received oppressive sentences. For example, Kemba Smith grew up in a loving middle-class home, actively participating in activities like Girl Scouts, gymnastics, ballet, and the high school band.[100] When she matriculated at Hampton University in Virginia, Smith began to suffer doubts about her appearance and popularity. That made her a perfect target for Peter Michael Hall, a flamboyant man eight years her elder, who spoke in a charming Jamaican accent, drove fancy cars, wore expensive clothes, and was all the rage at Hampton—despite the fact that he was not a college student. Instead, Hall was the kingpin of an East Coast drug ring that moved millions of dollars in cocaine during the 1980s and early 1990s.

After they began dating, Hall exerted more and more control over Smith, beating her repeatedly, threatening her life, telling her she couldn't leave, and using her as a "mule" in his drug business. When Smith eventually summoned the strength to leave, she returned home to her parents, pregnant with Hall's child, only to learn that she had been indicted for a variety of offenses, including conspiracy to distribute cocaine. Federal law enforcement authorities told Smith that the charges would be dropped if she would disclose the location of Hall, who was now on the U.S. Marshals' "15 Most-Wanted List." Unfortunately, Smith agreed to cooperate with the government only after Hall had been found dead in a Seattle apartment. With nothing to offer in exchange for a plea bargain, Smith

141

pled guilty to a number of charges and hoped for mercy from the prosecution or the court. None was forthcoming: The government failed to ask for a downward departure or some type of judicial leniency, and the trial judge hammered Smith with a staggering 294 month sentence. It didn't matter that Smith was a college student with a strong family background and promising future, had no prior record and had never personally sold drugs, had been abused and threatened by the chief culprit in the criminal scheme, and was the mother of an infant child. Under the Guidelines, none of that mattered: Smith would have to spend almost a quarter-century in federal prison, and her child would grow up in a parentless home.

The story of Clarence Aaron is just as disturbing. Aaron grew up in a poor section of Mobile, Alabama, raised by his grandfather, a shipyard worker who made it his foremost goal to ensure that his grandson received a college education. Under his grandfather's tutelage, Aaron was a successful high school athlete and student, and received an athletic scholarship to college. He was the first member of his family to attend a university, where he majored in marketing and participated in extracurricular activities. In the summer before his senior year, Aaron made the mistake of introducing two groups of drug dealers, for which he was paid $1,500. Months later, he was pulled out of class by FBI agents, arrested, and charged with conspiracy to distribute crack cocaine. Unknown to Aaron, the major players in the drug ring had already been arrested and were scheming to lay all blame on the then 23-year-old college athlete. But while the big fish in the drug ring were able to snitch out others down the proverbial food chain, Aaron had no information to provide law enforcement. "The only thing I did know was that I introduced the two parties," he lamented in a PBS interview, "but that's as far as I could give them. I couldn't give no name, no place, none of that and so . . . what could I do?"[101]

At trial, Aaron's former friends and even a cousin testified against him, claiming that he was the mastermind behind the drug ring. In return, prosecutors made "substantial assistance" motions in their favor that resulted in drastically reduced sentences. But when Aaron was convicted, there was no motion for a reduced sentence. Instead, prosecutors argued that he was responsible for distributing nine kilos of cocaine, which was subsequently converted into crack. The government had no independent evidence on the amount of drugs distributed, with only the word of snitches supporting the quantity and attached punishment. "Nobody ever saw any drugs," Aaron's attorney noted, "but because of what [the snitches] said the quantity was, and because of the Sentencing Guidelines we have in this country today, the sentencing judge had no alternative except to sentence Clarence Aaron to life without parole."[102] So Aaron sits in a federal cell today, a model prisoner, with no prior record and only a year away from a college degree. He admits it was wrong to introduce the two groups of drug dealers, but some say his biggest mistake was not playing ball with the government and telling the prosecutors what they wanted to hear. "Either tell the truth, probably go to prison for the rest of your life—or lie, cooperate with the government, do whatever it takes to get a lesser sentence," says Aaron in describing his Hobbesian choice. "Which sounds better?"[103]

Finally, consider the recent case of 38-year-old Dale Yirkovsky. While helping to remodel the home in which he was staying, Yirkovsky found a .22-caliber round and placed it in a small box in his room. Some time later, the police came to the home and asked to search Yirkovsky's room after his ex-girlfriend claimed that he still had some of her property. During the search, law enforcement turned up the single bullet, and Yirkovsky admitted "putting it in a safe place to keep it from being a public hazard."[104] According to the *Des Moines Register*, federal prosecutors "hoped to squeeze information out of Yirkovsky about other crimes," and although he pled guilty and cooperated, "the feds refused to reduce the severity of the charge."[105] On the basis of his prior record, Yirkovsky was convicted in federal court of being a felon in possession of ammunition and received an astonishing 15-year sentence. The appellate court affirmed the judgment, conceding that the prison term was "an extreme penalty under the facts," but ultimately concluding that "our hands are tied in this matter by the mandatory minimum sentence which Congress established."[106] Dissenting Judge Morris Arnold called the punishment "draconian" and maintained that "the severity of sentences in general under the United States Sentencing Guidelines and recent congressional enactments is, or ought to be, a matter of great public concern to every citizen."[107] Nonetheless, Dale Yirkovsky will be imprisoned for the next decade and a half for the crime of possessing a single bullet, with neither a gun nor criminal intent.

Judge as Judge: Sentencing beyond the Guidelines

As inequities under the Guidelines have become more apparent, plaguing nearly every federal courthouse, scholars, practitioners, and the media have joined the majority of federal trial judges in criticizing the Guidelines.[108] Even initial supporters of sentencing reform, such as Judge Jon Newman, have concluded that "these guidelines go far too far," creating a surreal world "like 'Alice in Wonderland.' "[109] Unfortunately, many of the most influential and eloquent critics seem to concede that the commission and its Guidelines are here to stay. For instance, Professor Stith and Judge Cabranes temper their compelling arguments for change with "a recognition that the Guidelines are likely to remain substantially intact for some time to come."[110]

Admittedly, the resources and labor put into the Guidelines, as well as the passage of time since their creation, pose significant barriers to any large-scale reform efforts. But, of course, the same could have been said about the great liquor ban of the early 20th century. As one senator put it in 1930, "There is as much chance of repealing [Prohibition] as there is for a humming-bird to fly to the planet Mars with the Washington Monument tied to its tail."[111] Yet just a few years later, America's ill-fated experiment in alcohol criminalization was over. With nearly 15 years of Guidelines sentencing under our collective belt, it's high time to consider alternatives to the current regime. Tinkering with the Guidelines will not do; in the words of one federal trial judge, the only remedy is to "tear it down and start all over."[112]

To begin with, architects of a new federal system of criminal justice should revisit the wisdom imparted by the previous generation of reformers but ignored by Congress and the commission—namely, the demand for code reform in addition to sentencing reform.[113] As pointed out in a 1977 Senate report:

> The need for extensive reform of the Federal criminal laws is apparent. Present statutory criminal law on the Federal level is often a hodgepodge of conflicting, contradictory, and imprecise laws with little relevance to each other or to the state of criminal law as a whole. It necessarily burdens the responsibility of assuring every man of knowing what he may do and what he may not do.[114]

Unfortunately, neither Congress nor the commission recognized that the concerns driving the reform movement—unwarranted sentencing disparities, for example, or general confusion on the purposes of punishment and the justification for a particular sentence—were not merely the function of indeterminate sentencing. Instead, various defects in the federal sentencing system could be traced back to the disorganized and virtually incomprehensible set of crimes dispersed throughout the federal code. Whether appreciated or not, defining crime and setting punishment work in unison, simultaneously describing banned conduct and calibrating its gravity. It is hard to imagine the crime of murder, for instance, without also visualizing the penalty—death or life in prison. The punishment is part of the crime's definition, conveying the seriousness of killing others with malice aforethought. An offense can no more be isolated from punishment than a story can be told without its conclusion.

Successful reform projects must also recognize that sentencing discretion is not an evil in itself. Instead, it is a tool that can be used for positive goals, like creatively structuring a sentence that fits both crime and criminal—or, conversely, for negative ends, such as secretly increasing punishment on the basis of the offender's race. Moreover, discretionary judgments that affect sentencing can be found throughout the criminal justice system, not just in the judicial branch. Such judgments include the legislature's definition of crime and possible punishment; law enforcement's decision to investigate and arrest; the prosecutor's determination to charge a defendant or add particular offenses; the jury's verdict and, sometimes, its sentencing recommendation; the trial court's imposition of sentence; an appellate court's review of that sentence; and the parole board's consideration of early release.

With those considerations in mind, reform of federal sentencing should begin by examining the entire process from a holistic perspective. As just suggested, it would reevaluate the current potpourri of crimes in the federal code, with an eye toward organizing penal statutes into a comprehendible statement of federal offenses and the principles of criminal liability. Successful reform efforts might also examine the process of selecting the actors who wield discretion, most notably Article III judges. The sentencing reform movement was driven by images of unduly lenient or severe jurists, mocked as either "turn 'em loose Bruce" or "hang 'em high Harry."[115] But

145

such caricatures, fostered by media hype and political opportunism, are belied by the reality of judicial appointments in the federal system. Article III judges are individually selected by the president, put through the rigmarole of Senate confirmation, and accorded life tenure and salary protection, all to ensure qualified and independent judges on the federal bench.[116] Given the multiple layers of investigation into their character and fitness, the men and women of the federal judiciary are probably the most qualified and trustworthy decisionmakers in national government and the precise individuals that the American public should entrust with the most important judgments in the criminal process. So if the existence of skilled trial courts is assumed—a justified premise, extremist nonsense to the contrary, given the current corps of district court judges[117]—sentencing reform efforts might build upon the following general ideas:

Shared discretion. American constitutional democracy demands that lawmakers define crime and potential punishment, juries decide guilt, and judges impose sentence. But this separation of powers and labor does not require that each body be hermetically sealed from the others. Instead, a healthy division would encourage some sharing of authority while securing each body sufficient discretion to adequately perform its tasks. So, for instance, juries might continue service after a determination of guilt, remaining for the sentencing hearing and then providing the judge with an advisory opinion on an appropriate punishment. In turn, legislators could set broad boundaries of punishment that accommodate the variations in crime and criminals, thereby ensuring trial judges sufficient discretion to render moral judgment through sentencing. The federal sentencing ranges under the "25 percent rule" are simply too narrow to account for relevant differences among cases. A better approach would create, with care and consideration, a sufficiently low sentencing floor for the "good" defendant and a sufficiently high ceiling for the hardcore criminal, regardless of the span between the two.[118]

Real guidelines. The Guidelines are in no way "guidelines," at least as the term is typically defined: a recommendation or general principle for decisionmaking. Instead, the Guidelines have become obligatory on the courts, with the commission even referring to their strictures as mandatory. A better approach would establish real guidelines for real judges, and once again, much can be learned from the wisdom of legal reformers from the recent past, such as Professor Kenneth Culp Davis. In his seminal book, *Discretionary Justice*, Professor Davis emphasized that "discretionary power is a necessary government tool but excessive discretionary power is dangerous and harmful." Rather than seeking its elimination, Davis argued that discretion should be confined, structured, and checked. For federal sentencing, this might suggest a system of benchmarks that provide starting points for judicial decisionmaking. Professor Alschuler has proposed a set of "recurring paradigmatic cases" that could provide standards for sentencing, such as the young, poor, and disadvantaged man who becomes a small-time drug dealer. Real guidelines would offer a presumptive punishment and rationale for this paradigmatic case while empowering trial courts to set a different sentence on the basis of facts that distinguish the present case from the benchmark. A necessary consequence of real guidelines would be the end of the 258-box federal sentencing grid and the low comedy it produces. Derisively analogized to the games Parcheesi and "GO," the sentencing grid will not be missed by many.[119]

Written reasons, appellate review, and institutional memory. A system of real guidelines might foster a common law of sentencing in federal courts, with the reasoned judgments of past decisions helping trial judges decide today's cases. At a minimum, the common law model requires three ingredients for success. First, trial judges should provide written reasons for the sentences they pronounce, explaining to the defendant and all others the exact justifications for a particular punishment. Second, appellate courts should be able to review a sentence to ensure reasonable application of real guidelines, a justified deviation from the guidelines, and the absence of invidious discrimination against the defendant. And third, the written reasons and relevant appellate decisions should be part of an institutional memory for the federal judiciary, allowing future courts to use these judgments as a database for their sentencing decisions. In 1999, Professor Ronald Wright pointed out that Scottish judges have computer access to key information about recent sentences: "When the time arrives to impose a sentence, the judge asks the database to display information about cases that resemble the case at hand in all relevant ways ... [and] the database then informs the judge about the sentences imposed in past cases with comparable features, including information about the distribution of the sentences imposed."[120] It is somewhat embarrassing that computer-savvy Americans were not the first to consider this humane use of technology.

Full transparency. Finally, whatever model eventually replaces the Guidelines should generate an honest system of sentencing. The current process encourages judicial sleight of hand and fact bargaining by the parties, resulting in "facts" that are not factual and legal rulings that push the envelope of reasonable interpretation. To be sure, the outcome of an individual case may be acceptable, avoiding draconian punishment under the Guidelines. But collectively, this chicanery by judges and attorneys only undermines the moral authority of law and calls into question a system that tolerates systemic deception. "Our government is the potent, the omnipresent teacher," Justice Louis Brandeis famously observed, and "if the government becomes a lawbreaker, it breeds contempt for law."[121] Unfortunately, the Guidelines teach that circumventing the law is acceptable, as long as it is done under the table and then masked above with passable lies. Needless to say, no legitimate form of government would perform in such a manner.

Together, shared discretion and real guidelines coupled with written reasons, appellate review, institutional memory, and full transparency would help create a federal common law of sentencing that treats offenders as human beings—worthy of individualized treatment and a comprehensible justification for their fate—while limiting the potential for unwarranted disparities in punishment. The discretion allowed under nonmandatory real guidelines would permit judges to tailor punishment to the unique characteristics of a given offender rather than cramming the offender into a sentencing pigeonhole on the basis of a truncated list of factors. In turn, written reasons, appellate review, and institutional memory would ensure that punishment is not determined by the courthouse door one enters but rather by a just assessment of the offense and offender in light of punishment received by similarly situated criminals. Finally, full transparency would guarantee the bona fides of sentencing information and judgments, both in the aggregate and for specific cases. In this way, a new system of sentencing could navigate between the Scylla of arbitrariness in the indeterminate sentencing era and the Charybdis of excessive uniformity under today's mandatory Guidelines.

Conclusion

Kemba Smith—formerly federal inmate No. 26370-083, serving a 24-year sentence under the Guidelines—recently graduated from Virginia Union University with a 3.1 grade point average. Since her release from prison, Smith has reconnected with her now seven-year-old son, completed her bachelor's degree, worked part-time as a legal assistant and social work intern, and recounted her story at public forums and college campuses, warning other young people about the dangers of drugs and drug dealers. She has now set her sights on becoming a lawyer. "It just seems right for me to pursue law," Smith says, "to have that title to go along with my advocacy."[122] After six years in prison, she is now ready to follow her dreams and provide for her family.

But neither the Guidelines nor the commission set Smith free; no judge or prosecutor was able to undo the draconian sentence that had been levied against this first-time, low-level offender. Instead, the 30-year-old mother, who had been caught in an abusive relationship with a drug kingpin, received mercy from a most unlikely source. At the end of his term, President Bill Clinton included Smith on a much ridiculed list of offenders who received executive pardons. Yet Smith's case is the exception proving the rule—the futility of trying to remedy excesses and injustices under the Guidelines without also changing the current sentencing system itself. Only a tiny fraction of pardon applications actually receive substantive review and an even smaller amount are granted by the president.[123] The number is likely to dwindle even further under the Bush administration, with the pardon fiasco of fugitive financier Marc Rich still fresh in the mind of the electorate.

More important, an infrequently used, postconviction approach cannot even start to ameliorate the harsh punishment demanded by the Guidelines. As suggested by the head of the NAACP's criminal justice project, "Kemba is . . . just the tip of the iceberg."[124] Clarence Aaron and Dale Yirkovsky will remain in federal lockup, as will countless other low-level and first-time offenders who received cruel sentences under the Guidelines. They were punished not by the respective trial courts, but by a process that prevents moral judgment. Absent a repeal of the Guidelines, many more defendants will follow them into prison, fodder for the thoughtless machine that is federal sentencing.[125]

American conceptions of justice demand that the Guidelines be scrapped and the commission disbanded. Congress created an unconstitutional "fourth branch" of government, with the commission assuming the power to make law but lacking any type of political accountability. Moreover, the commission has usurped much of the judiciary's traditional authority over sentencing through its enactment of mandatory Guidelines that all but eliminate the capacity of trial courts to mete out individualized punishment. In turn, the current system has drastically expanded the power of federal prosecutors, giving them yet another tool with which to squeeze out information and guilty pleas from defendants while encouraging law enforcement to play fast-and-loose with the rules of evidence.

The Guidelines have also undermined the legitimacy of sentencing law, diluting and obscuring moral judgment. The complexity of the current system generates confusion among both criminal justice actors and lay citizens, while the hypertechnical character of the Guidelines produces sentencing variations that are nearly impossible to justify. The Guidelines also dehumanize the process of punishment by deeming relevant only certain factors about the offense or offender and ignoring all others, mechanically plugging into the sentencing equation those privileged characteristics and then spitting out the bottom line of punishment.

To temper the severity of federal sentencing, prosecutors, defense attorneys, and even judges have engaged in the hidden nullification of the Guidelines, tinkering with case facts, for instance, to reach an agreeable sentence. Although this nullification may lead to just outcomes in particular cases, the process of fact bargaining engages the parties in blatant dishonesty, unbecoming to officers of the court. This corruption not only subverts the moral authority of the federal system, but also conflicts with the democratic prerequisites of open and accountable government. As a result, many practitioners, jurists, and even average citizens have come to view the Guidelines with cynicism and contempt.

There are many possible paths to positive change, all leading to the dissolution of the commission and the repeal of its Guidelines. Brave members of Congress might step up to the plate of their own accord, recognizing the injustice of the current system and instigating a new era of sentencing reform. A blue-ribbon commission, representing all parties with a stake in federal sentencing, could be impaneled and empowered to design an approach to punishment that avoids the Guidelines' many vices. It's even possible that the citizenry itself might grow weary of the enormous financial and human costs, placing pressure on Congress to scrap the Guidelines and start again.

In the end, the American people must decide whether defendants should be sentenced by the complex, hypertechnical rules of a mechanical process—or, instead, by an entity capable of individualized decisions made pursuant to wisdom and experience. If the last 15 years have proved anything, it is that justice in sentencing cannot be served by the convoluted rules of a distant bureaucracy. Only trial judges can mete out punishment that fits both the offense and the offender, mindful of the deeply held notion that people must be treated as unique beings worthy of individualized treatment and not as undifferentiated objects on the conveyor belt of sentencing. Ultimately, Congress must end the Guidelines era and begin anew, guaranteeing that the next 15 years of federal punishment will not be like the last. It is time to scrap the commission and its Guidelines, and to embark on a new age of moral judgment in sentencing.

This is an abridged version of a study originally published as Cato Institute Policy Analysis no. 458, November 1, 2002.

Notes

1. See Bureau of Justice Statistics, *1999 Sourcebook of Criminal Justice Statistics* (Washington: Government Printing Office, 2000), p. 500.

2. See Erik Luna, "Drug Exceptionalism," *Villanova Law Review* 47 (2002): 770.

3. See *1999 Sourcebook*, p. 526.

4. Ibid., p. 442.

5. See, for example, Paul D. Borman, "The Federal Sentencing Guidelines," *Thomas M. Cooley Law Review* 16 (1999): 4.

6. Michael Tonry, *Sentencing Matters* (New York: Oxford University Press, 1966), p. 83. See also Michael Tonry, "'Mandatory Minimum Penalties and the U.S. Sentencing Commission's 'Mandatory Guidelines,' " *Federal Sentencing Reporter* 4 (1991): 129.

7. See *Special Report*, p. ii; U.S. Sentencing Commission, *Annual Report—1990* (Washington: U.S. Sentencing Commission, 1991), p. 1.

8. José A. Cabranes, "Sentencing Guidelines: A Dismal Failure," *New York Law Journal* (February 11, 1992): 2; *United States v. Harrington*, 947 F.2d 956, 964 (1991) (Edwards, J., concurring); and Lawrence Karlton, "Commentary," *Federal Sentencing Reporter* 4 (November/December 1991): 186.

9. G. Thomas Esele, "The Sentencing Guidelines System? No. Sentencing Guidelines? Yes." *Federal Probation* (December 1991): 20.

10. Ibid., p. 21 (quoting Judge Donald Lay).

11. Federal Courts Study Committee, *Report of the Federal Courts Study Committee* (Washington: Administrative Office of the U.S. Courts, 1990), pp. 133–44.

12. Federal Judicial Center, *The United States Sentencing Guidelines: Results of the Federal Judicial Center's 1996 Survey* (Washington: Federal Judicial Center, 1997); Federal Judicial Center, *Planning for the Future: Results of a 1992 Federal Judicial Center Survey of United States Judges* (Washington: Federal Judicial Center, 1994). See also Don J. DeBenedictis, "The Verdict Is In," *American Bar Association Journal* 79 (1993): 78.

13. For brief historical reviews of federal sentencing, see Kate Stith and José A. Cabranes, *Fear of Judging: Sentencing Guidelines in the Federal Courts* (Chicago: University of Chicago Press, 1998), pp. 9–22; Douglas A. Berman, "Balanced and Purposeful Departures: Fixing a Jurisprudence That Undermines the Federal Sentencing Guidelines," *Notre Dame Law Review* 76 (2000): 25–30; Kate Stith and José A. Cabranes, "Judging under the Federal Sentencing Guidelines," *Northwestern University Law Review* 91 (1997): 1248–54; and William J. Powell and Michael T. Cimino, "Prosecutorial Discretion under the Federal Sentencing Guidelines: Is the Fox Guarding the Hen House?" *West Virginia Law Review* 97 (1995): 374–379.

14. See, for example, Marvin E. Frankel, *Criminal Sentences: Law without Order* (New York: Hill and Wang, 1973); Marvin E. Frankel, "Lawlessness in Sentencing," *University of Cincinnati Law Review* 41 (1972): 1; Marvin E. Frankel, "Sentencing Guidelines: A Need for Creative Collaboration," *Yale Law Journal* 101 (1992): 2043.

15. See Stith and Cabranes, *Fear of Judging*, pp. 30–31; Michael Tonry, "Twenty Years of Sentencing Reform: Steps Forward, Steps Backward," Judicature 78 (1995): 170.

16. See Stith and Cabranes, *Fear of Judging*, p. 31; Berman, pp. 26–28; Powell and Cimino, p. 379; Frankel, "Sentencing Guidelines," pp. 2044–45; Charles J. Ogletree Jr., "The Death of Discretion? Reflections on the Federal Sentencing Guidelines," *Harvard Law Review* 101 (1988): 1942–44; Daniel J. Freed, "Federal Sentencing in the Wake of Guidelines: Unacceptable Limits on the Discretion of Sentencers," *Yale Law Journal* 101 (1992): 1688–89; José A. Cabranes, "A Failed Utopian Experiment," *National Law Journal*, July 27, 1992, p. 17.

17. See, for example, Stith and Cabranes, *Fear of Judging*, pp. 106–12.

18. Frankel, *Criminal Sentences*, p. 49.

19. Ibid., p. 5.

20. Ibid., pp.118–24.

21. Ibid., p. 114.

22. Ibid., p. 113.

23. Ibid., p. 115.

24. See Mary Pat Flaherty and Joan Biskupic, "Despite Overhaul, Federal Sentencing Still Misfires," *Washington Post*, October 6, 1996.

25. Statement of Senator Kennedy, *Congressional Record* (September 30, 1982) 128, p. S12,784.

26. See Stith and Cabranes, *Fear of Judging*, pp. 43–47; Ogletree, p. 1944 n.35.

27. See Stith and Cabranes, *Fear of Judging*, pp. 47–48; Flaherty and Biskupic, "Despite Overhaul, Federal Sentencing Still Misfires," *Washington Post*, October 6, 1996."

28. See 18 U.S.C. § 3553 (a) (2000); Senate Committee on the Judiciary, Comprehensive Crime Control Act of 1983, 98th Cong. 1st sess., 1983, S. Rept. No. 225, 1, 39, reprinted in 1984 U.S.C.C.A.N. 3182, 3222.

29. 28 U.S.C. § 991 (2000).

30. 28 U.S.C.A. § 994(b)(2) (2000).

31. 28 U.S.C.A. § 994(d) (2000).

32. 28 U.S.C. § 991(a) (2000).

33. *Mistretta v. United States*, 488 U.S. 361 (1989).

34. Ibid., p. 427 (Scalia, J., dissenting).

35. Ibid.

36. Ibid., pp. 414–15.

37. U.S. Constitution, art. I, sec. 1.

38. See 28 U.S.C. § 994(p) (2000).

39. See S. Rept. 225, pp. 3363–64; *United States v. Lopez*, 938 F.2d 1293, 1297 (1991); Stith and Cabranes, *Fear of Judging*, pp. 40, 56–57, 95; Stith and Cabranes, "Judging Under," pp. 1271–72.

40. U.S. Sentencing Commission, *Supplementary Report on the Initial Sentencing Guidelines and Policy Statements* (Washington: U.S. Sentencing Commission, 1987), p. 19.

41. *Mistretta*, at 396.

42. See, for example, Stith and Cabranes, *Fear of Judging*, p. 48; Tonry, *Sentencing Matters*, p. 84; Ogletree, p. 1948; and Jeffrey S. Parker and Michael K. Block, "The Limits of Federal Criminal Sentencing Policy; Or Confessions of Two Reformed Reformers," *George Mason Law Review* 9 (2001): 1019.

43. See, for example, Stith and Cabranes, *Fear of Judging*, p. 48 (arguing that "the U.S. Sentencing Commission from its inception has been highly visible to bar and bench, acutely sensitive to the political environment in which it operates, and controversial"); Tonry, *Sentencing Matters*, p. 84 (noting that the Commission's "work was highly politicized from the outset, and it was riven by ideological factionalism and political intrigue.")

44. Parker and Block, p. 1019. Michael Block "was an initial member of the Commission, serving from its inception in 1985 until 1989." Ibid., p. 1003 n.13.

45. Stith and Cabranes, *Fear of Judging*, p. 95.

46. See Parker and Block, pp. 1022–25.

47. Albert W. Alschuler, "The Failure of Sentencing Guidelines: A Plea for Less Aggregation," *University of Chicago Law Review* 58 (1991): 926.

48. Ibid.

49. Robert F. Howe, "Drug Sentencing Faulted; Benefits for Snitches Leave Some Out in Cold," *Washington Post*, February 25, 1991.

50. Quoted in ibid. See also Mary Pat Flaherty and Joan Biskupic, "Prosecutors Can Stack the Deck; Sentencing Powers Shift from Judges," *Washington Post*, October 7, 1996 (discussing sentencing disparity between two brothers based on cooperation with prosecutors); and *United States v. Ives*, 984 F.2d 649 (1993) (same).

51. *U.S. Sentencing Guidelines Manual* § 1B1.3(a)(2) (2000).

52. The results can be stunning and disconcerting, with undercover agents encouraging suspects to act in ways that increase their own punishment through a process of "sentence entrapment" or "sentence manipulation." Federal officials are particularly notorious for structuring arrests to maximize the number of guns or drugs that can be pinned on a suspect. See Flaherty and Biskupic, "Prosecutors Can Stack the Deck," p. A1. One agent even persuaded a drug defendant to convert her cocaine from powder to crack, upping her sentence exponentially. See *United States v. Shepherd*, 857 F.Supp. 105 (D.D.C. 1994), vacated by 102 F.3d 558 (D.C. Cir. 1996).

53. See *United States v. Watts*, 519 U.S. 148 (1997).

54. Stith and Cabranes, *Fear of Judging*, p. 140, citing Brief of Appellee, pp.17–18, *United States v. Fulton*, No. 96–1029 (1996). See *United States v. Fulton*, 173 F.3d 847, 1999 WL 132172 (upholding upward departure based on proof of murder).

55. *United States v. Tejada*, 956 F.2d 1256 (1992).

56. See, for example, *United States v. Ebbole*, 917 F.2d 1495, 1495–96 (1990) (increase from one gram to 1.7 kilograms of cocaine).

57. 67 F.3d 1312 (1995).

58. On the third day of deliberations, "the jury sent a note to the court: 'Honorable Judge Curran, the jury is unable to reach a unanimous verdict, in spite of intense discussion and all of the information provided by the court. How do we proceed?' " Ibid., at. 1318. According to reviewing judge Richard Posner, "the jurors were actually rather troubled by the issue of guilt—enough so that the judge had to give [a special instruction] to blast a verdict out of them." *United States v. Rodriguez*, 73 F.3d 161, 162 (1996) (Posner, J., dissenting).

59. 73 F.3d at 162.

60. John Griffiths, "Ideology in Criminal Procedure or 'A Third Model' of the Criminal Process," *Yale Law Journal* 79 (1970): 359 (describing the "Battle Model" of the criminal process).

61. Stith and Cabranes, *Fear of Judging*, p. 5.

62. See, for example, Flaherty and Biskupic, "Despite Overhaul."

63. Mary Pat Flaherty, "Innocent Errors" (quoting Judge John Rhodes); Tonry, *Sentencing Matters*, pp. 98–99.

64. Stephen Breyer, "Federal Sentencing Guidelines Revisited," *Federal Sentencing Reporter* 11 (1999): 180. Some lines that have been drawn by the Guidelines "seem crazy" and "loony," such as counting the weight of the carrier medium impregnated with LSD in determining the sentencing range. *United States v. Marshall*, 908 F.2d 1312, 1332, 1333 (7th Cir. 1990) (Posner, J., dissenting). Under the initial Guidelines, a first-time offender caught selling 100 doses of LSD in sugar cubes would receive a sentence of between 188 and 235 months. But if he had sold his stash on blotter paper, his punishment would decrease to 63–78 months; if he sold the LSD in gelatin capsules, his sentence would have been 27–33 months; and if he sold the drug in pure form, he would have received a term of just 10–16 months. See *Chapman v. United States*, 500 U.S. 453, 458 n.2 (1991). In each scenario, the amount of intoxicant peddled remains the same, only the length of imprisonment changes. Although the Supreme Court somehow found this scheme "rational" (ibid., pp. 465–66), the commission eventually changed the Guidelines to limit the carrier medium's effect on sentences for LSD-related crimes. *U.S. Sentencing Guidelines Manual* § 2D1.1; ibid., App. C. Nonetheless, LSD offenders continue to receive lengthy sentences, based in part on the carrier medium, with little chance of mercy. See *United States v. Camacho*, 261 F.3d 1071 (11th Cir. 2001) (LSD offender resentenced under amended Guidelines); *United States v. Sia*, 104 F.3d 348, 1996 WL 728191 (1st Cir.) (same).

65. Flaherty and Biskupic, "Despite Overhaul" (quoting Judge Samuel Kent).

66. Joan Biskupic and Mary Pat Flaherty, "Loss of Discretion Fuels Frustration on Federal Bench; Most District Judges Want Shift in Sentencing Rules," *Washington Post*, October 8, 1996 (quoting Judge Judith Keep).

67. Remarks of Hon. Morris E. Lasker, U.S. District Judge for the Southern District of New York, before the Symposium on Sentencing Guidelines, September 9, 1997, www.november.org/dissentingopinions/Lasker.html. The Guideline's "mechanical jurisprudence" or "sentencing by the numbers," as some jurists have called it, converts a judge as moral actor into an "automaton," "rubber-stamp bureaucrat," "notary public," or "accountant." See "Summary of Proceedings," p. 2054 (comments of Judge Edward Becker); Cabranes, "Failed Utopian Experiment," p. 17; Stith and

Cabranes, *Fear of Judging*, p. 169; Weinstein, p. 364; Frank S. Gilbert, "The Probation Officer's Perception of the Allocation of Discretion," *Federal Sentencing Reporter* 4 (1991): 109; and Ellsworth A.Van Graafeiland, "Some Thoughts on the Sentencing Reform Act of 1984," *Villanova Law Review* 31 (1986): 1293–94. See also *United States v. Russell*, 685 F.Supp. 1245, 1249 (N.D. Ga. 1988) ("[The Guidelines] reduce the role of the sentencing judge to filling in the blanks and applying a rigid, mechanical formula."); *United States v. Justice*, 877 F.2d 664, 666 (8th Cir. 1989) ("sentencing has been relegated to a somewhat mechanical process"); *United States v. Bogle*, 689 F.Supp. 1121, 1163 (S.D. Fla. 1988) (Aronovitz, J., concurring) (describing federal sentencing as a "mechanistic administrative formula"). In the end, laments Judge Weinstein, the Guidelines "tend to deaden the sense that a judge must treat each defendant as a unique human being." Weinstein, p. 366.

68. Utah Code Annotated, (Lexis Law Publishing, 1982), secs. 76-5-103, 76-3-203.
69. Cal. Penal Code, sec. 245(a)(2).
70. 18 U.S.C. § 111(b) (2000).
71. *U.S. Sentencing Guidelines Manual* 2A2.2(b)(2)(C).
72. The Guidelines' limited leeway might be more palatable if trial judges had ample means to depart from the initial sentencing range, but commission interpretations and appellate rulings have confined departures to two circumstances. First, prosecutors can request a downward departure from the sentencing range based on the defendant's substantial assistance. The decision to seek this type of departure rests solely with the government, however, and provides no independent discretionary authority for the district court. The second basis for departure is where the judge finds a factor "not adequately taken into consideration" by the commission, requiring a sentence different from that prescribed by the Guidelines, 18 U.S.C. § 3553(b) (2000). The relevant statutory provision was intended to provide a type of safety valve for the courts to deal with unique situations that fall outside the "heartland" of cases amenable to a given sentencing range. See *U.S. Sentencing Guidelines Manual* § 1A4.b ("The Commission intends the sentencing courts to treat each guideline as carving out a 'heartland,' a set of typical cases embodying the conduct that each guideline describes. . . . When a court finds an atypical case, one to which a particular guideline linguistically applies but where the conduct significantly differs from the norm, the court may consider whether a departure is warranted."). Unfortunately, the commission has determined that departures from the heartland should be "rare," in large part because most circumstances have already been considered and either incorporated into the Guidelines or expressly rejected. Wary of this alleged preemption, the federal appellate courts have been downright miserly in foreclosing heartland-based departures. See *United States v. Weinberger*, 91 F.3d 642, 644 (4th Cir. 1996) ("Given the comprehensive sentencing structure embodied in the guidelines, '[o]nly rarely will we conclude that a factor was not adequately taken into consideration by the Commission.' ").
73. *Wisconsin v. Mitchell*, 508 U.S. 476, 484 (1993).
74. 28 U.S.C. § 994(d) (2000).
75. *U.S. Sentencing Guidelines Manual* § 5H1.1 (age); § 5H1.2 (education and vocational skills); § 5H1.3 (mental and emotional conditions); § 5H1.4 (physical condition, including drug or alcohol dependence or abuse); § 5H1.5 (employment record); § 5H1.6 (family ties and responsibilities, and community ties); § 5H1.11 (prior good works, including military, civic, charitable, or public service); § 5H1.12 (lack of guidance as a youth).

76. Alschuler, p. 902.

77. See Tonry, *Sentencing Matters*, pp. 11, 72–99.

78. See Stephen J. Schulhofer, "Assessing the Federal Sentencing Process: The Problem Is Uniformity, Not Disparity," *American Criminal Law Review* 29 (1992): 835, 851–70.

79. Ilene H. Nagel, "Foreword: Structuring Sentencing Discretion: The New Federal Sentencing Guidelines," *Journal of Criminal Law and Criminology* 80 (1990): 883, 934.

80. See *United States v. Rodriguez*, 724 F.Supp. 1118, 1122 (1989).

81. Ibid.

82. See Biskupic and Flaherty, "Loss of Discretion," p. A1 (comparing sentences for drug offender and murderer). But see Erik Luna, "The Prohibition Apocalypse," *DePaul Law Review* 46 (1997): 485 ("Former 'drug czar' William Bennett would behead drug dealers. Nancy Reagan branded casual users 'accomplice[s] to murder,' and the erstwhile police chief of Los Angeles, Daryl Gates, opined that even occasional drug users should be 'taken out and shot.' ").

83. Flaherty and Biskupic, "Prosecutors Can Stack the Deck," (quoting James Druker).

84. See, for example, Catherine M. Goodwin, "The Independent Role of the Probation Officer at Sentencing and in Applying *Koon v. United States*," Federal Probation, September 1996, p. 71.

85. Flaherty and Biskupic, "Prosecutors Can Stack the Deck."

86. Tony Garoppolo, "Fact Bargaining: What the Sentencing Commission Hath Wrought," *BNA Criminal Practice Manual* 10 (1996): 405. See also Eugene D. Natali, "The Probation Officer, Bean Counting and Truth in Sentencing," *Federal Sentencing Reporter* 4 (1991): 103 ("Subtle and creative forces began to short-circuit the whole process of guideline sentencing. Attorneys for the defense and the government found new ways to ply their old trade with plea bargains . . . in all shapes and sizes . . . stipulations seemed to be fiction writings, when compared with the known facts of the cases they attempted to address.").

87. Probation Officers Advisory Group, "Probation Officers Advisory Group Survey," *Federal Sentencing Reporter* 8 (1996): 303.

88. See Stephen J. Schulhofer and Ilene H. Nagel, "Plea Negotiations under the Federal Sentencing Guidelines: Guideline Circumvention and Its Dynamics in the Post-*Mistretta* Period," *Northwestern University Law Review* 91 (1997): 1284; Ilene H. Nagel and Stephen J. Schulhofer, "A Tale of Three Cities: An Empirical Study of Charging and Bargaining Practices under the Federal Sentencing Guidelines," *Southern California Law Review* 66 (1992): 501.

89. *United States v. Rodriguez*, 162 F.3d 135, 150–52 (1998).

90. Ibid., at 152.

91. *Berthoff v. United States*, 140 F.Supp.2d 50, 66 (D.Mass. 2001) (discussing *Rodriguez*).

92. Ibid., at 66, 90–91.

93. Flaherty and Biskupic, "Prosecutors Can Stack the Deck" (quoting Larry Silverman).

94. Schulhofer and Nagel, "Guideline Circumvention," p. 1312.

95. Weinstein, p. 365 (quoting anonymous federal judge).

96. See Erik Luna, "Transparent Policing," *Iowa Law Review* 85 (2000): 1154–63 (discussing trust of government, perceived legitimacy, and compliance with the law).

97. See generally Louis D. Brandeis, *Other People's Money* (1933): 62 ("Publicity is justly commended as a remedy for social and industrial disease. . . . Sunlight is said to be the best of disinfectants; electric light the most efficient policeman.")

98. See, for example, Stith and Cabranes, *Fear of Judging*, pp. 7, 104–142; Berman, pp. 61–65; Frank O. Bowman and Michael Heise, "Quiet Rebellion II: An Empirical Analysis of Declining Federal Drug Sentences Including Data from the District Level," *Iowa Law Review* 87 (2002): 477; Frank O. Bowman and Michael Heise, "Quiet Rebellion? Explaining Nearly a Decade of Declining Federal Drug Sentences," *Iowa Law Review* 86 (2001): 1054; John S. Martin Jr., "The Role of the Departure Power in Reducing Injustice and Unwarranted Disparity under the Sentencing Guidelines," *Brooklyn Law Review* 66 (2000): 259; James Anderson, Jeffrey Kling, and Kate Stith, "Measuring Interjudge Sentencing Disparity: Before and After the Federal Sentencing Guidelines," *Journal of Law and Economics* 42 (1999): 271; Schulhofer and Nagel, "Guideline Circumvention," p. 1284; Nagel and Schulhofer, "A Tale of Three Cities," p. 501; Gerald W. Heaney, "The Reality of Guidelines Sentencing: No End to Disparity," *American Criminal Law Review* 28 (1991): 161; and Stephen J. Schulhofer and Ilene H. Nagel, "Negotiated Pleas under the Federal Sentencing Guidelines: The First Fifteen Months," *American Criminal Law Review* 27 (1989): 231.

99. For purposes of clarification, I should make clear my own opinion on drugs and drug crime. As a civil libertarian on issues of criminal justice, I oppose prohibition as being immoral in theory, racist and classist in practice, and ultimately destined for failure in a free society. But being a civil libertarian doesn't demand sympathy or even tolerance for drug criminals such as defendant Rodriguez. Here is an individual who violates drug laws not for his own consumption or addiction. Rodriguez is not distributing marijuana to ease the pain of those who suffer from debilitating diseases like cancer and glaucoma. Nor is he a street-level drug offender who engages in crime as part of the reality of being a poor, young, minority male in today's inner cities. Instead, Rodriguez is the heir to gangster rumrunners like Al Capone, becoming rich through a failed government policy and demonstrating only indifference to the larger consequences of his criminality. In all likelihood, the identity of the contraband—whether it be booze or drugs or guns or whatever—is irrelevant to organized criminals such as Capone and Rodriguez. If the national ban on narcotics were lifted, such entrepreneurs would find another way to partake in the heightened financial margins of illegal commerce. So just as those who opposed alcohol prohibition in the early 20th century were not chums of Capone, modern-day civil libertarians need not befriend Rodriguez.

100. For descriptions of the Smith case, see Libby Copeland, "Kemba Smith's Hard Time," *Washington Post*, February 13, 2000; Reginald Stuart, "Justice Denied: Kemba's Nightmare Continues," *Emerge*, May 31, 2000, p. 41; and Reginald Stuart, "Kemba's Nightmare," *Emerge*, May 31, 1996, p. 28.

101. PBS, "Snitch," *Frontline* special, www.pbs.org/wgbh/frontline/shows/snitch/cases/aaron.html.

102. "Time to Rethink the War on Drugs?" Cato Institute Policy Forum, May 22, 2001, p. 11 (quoting criminal defense attorney Dennis Knizely).

103. PBS.

104. Dale Yirkovsky, "Letters to the Editor," *Des Moines Register*, February 11, 2002.

105. Register Editorial Board, "One Bullet, 15 Years," *Des Moines Register*, January 21, 2002.

106. *United States v. Yirkovsky*, 259 F.3d 704, 707 n.4 (2001).

107. *United States v. Yirkovsky*, 276 F.3d 384, 385 (2001) (Morris, J., dissenting).

108. "The Commission has been the Rodney Dangerfield of federal agencies: it 'don't get no respect.' Despised by judges, sneered at by scholars, ignored by the Justice Department, its guidelines circumvented by practitioners and routinely lambasted in the press, the Commission has, most alarmingly, fallen out of favor with the Congress that created it." Ronald Welch, "The Battle against Mandatory Minimums: A Report from the Front Lines," *Federal Sentencing Reporter* 9 (1996): 97.

109. Biskupic and Flaherty, "Loss of Discretion." See also *United States v. Galloway*, 976 F.2d 414, 438 (1992) (Bright, J., dissenting) ("Only in the world of Alice in Wonderland, in which up is down and down is up, and words lose their real meaning, does such a sentence comply with the Constitution.").

110. Stith and Cabranes, *Fear of Judging*, p. xi. This resignation to the current scheme is evidenced by, among other things, the modest nature of proposed congressional reforms. One bill (S. 1834) attempts to alleviate the grave sentencing disparity between crack and powder cocaine, increasing the amount of crack while simultaneously decreasing the quantity of powder cocaine that trigger mandatory minimum sentences. Another bill (H.R. 1978) would simply eliminate mandatory minimums for most drug crime. Both proposals offer improvements over the current approach to narcotics offenses, a major source of discontent in federal sentencing. But neither bill contemplates a change to the basic Guidelines scheme and its impediments to moral judgment by trial judges.

111. Luna, "The Prohibition Apocalypse," p. 564 (quoting Texas Sen. Morris Shepard).

112. Flaherty, "Innocent Errors" (quoting Judge John Rhodes).

113. See, for example, Frank J. Remington, "The Federal Sentencing Guidelines as a Criminal Code: Why the Model Penal Code Approach Is Preferable," *Federal Sentencing Reporter* 7 (1994): 116.

114. Criminal Code Reform Act of 1977, 95th Cong., 1st sess., 1977, S. Rept. 95–605, p. 3.

115. See Powell and Cimino, p. 379.

116. See *United States v. Boshell*, 728 F.Supp. 632, 637 (1990): "Regardless of which political party holds sway, the process for selecting federal judges is much the same. Nominees are hung out like fresh meat to be poked, prodded and examined in minute detail as to every aspect of their personal and professional lives. The first step is to gain the confidence of a nominating senator who will conduct such investigation as he deems appropriate. Then the FBI, Department of Justice, the American Bar Association, and the Judiciary Committee get into the act. Only after surviving scrutiny that far will the Senate consider granting its stamp of approval."

117. See ibid. "Judges may . . . occasionally ascend the bench without the basic qualifications to serve, but when the system fails in that manner, it is aberrational in the extreme."

118. Ronald F. Wright, "Rules for Sentencing Revolutions," *Yale Law Journal* 108 (1999): 1372–79 (discussing jury sentencing).

119. Kenneth Culp Davis, *Discretionary Justice: A Preliminary Inquiry* (Baton Rouge: Louisiana State University Press, 1969), p. 27; See Alschuler, pp. 939–49; Biskupic and Flaherty, "Loss of Discretion" (quoting Judge Bruce Selya: "People think of it as a game, like Parcheesi."); Marc Miller, "True Grid: Revealing Sentencing Policy," *U.C. Davis Law Review* 25 (1992): 588 n. 4 ("The table looks like the board for the game of 'GO.' ").

120. Wright, p. 1386.

121. *Olmstead v. United States*, 277 U.S. 438, 485 (1928) (Brandeis, J., dissenting).

122. See Kevin O'Hanlon, "Judge to Ask President Bush to Pardon Drug Dealer," *Associated Press*, January 9, 2002; Deborah Alexander, "Ruling Forces Judge to Impose Longer Sentence," *Omaha World-Herald*, January 9, 2002, p. B4; Deborah Alexander, "Court May Review Dealer's Sentence," *Omaha World-Herald*, September 4, 2001, p. B4; "Man Sentenced in Meth Case," *Tulsa World*, June 2, 1998, p. 5; Editorial, "Judge Not," *Tulsa World*, January 17, 1998, p. 16; Doug P. Grow, "Woman Is a Footnote in U.S. War on Drugs," *Minneapolis–St. Paul Star Tribune*, April 25, 2001, p. B2; Paul Gustafson, "First-time Offender Pleads to Lesser Offense, Gets 8 Years," *Minneapolis–St. Paul Star Tribune*, April 25, 2001, p. B2; "Judge Quits Case over Federal Sentencing Guidelines," *Associated Press*, January 20, 2001.

123. See, for example, *1999 Sourcebook*, p. 475.

124. Quoted in Stuart, "Kemba's Nightmare Continues."

125. Quoted in "Graduation puts 'Kemba's Nightmare' Further in the Past," *Associated Press*, May 10, 2002; and Michael Paul Williams, "Nightmare Shaped a Dream," *Richmond Times-Dispatch*, May 10, 2002.

Contributors

James V. DeLong is a senior fellow at the Progress & Freedom Foundation, where he directs the Center for the Study of Digital Property. He is also the author of *Property Matters: How Property Rights Are Under Assault—And Why You Should Care* (New York, NY Free Press, 1997).

Gene Healy is senior editor at the Cato Institute.

Erik Luna, formerly a state prosecutor and Fulbright Scholar on sentencing alternatives, is associate professor of law at the University of Utah College of Law.

Timothy Lynch is director of the Cato Institute's Project on Criminal Justice.

Grace-Marie Turner is president of the Galen Institute, a not-for-profit research organization that focuses on consumer-driven health care solutions.

Index

enforcement expense, 30–31
evidentiary standards and, 27
guidelines and standards for
invoking levels of prosecution,
22–24
individual and vicarious liability
considerations, 24–25
insolence toward, 22
license to trespass, 53–56
Environmental punitive sanctions/
measures
analysis of trend in applying, 14–17
civil justice system problems and
reforms, 39–40
command-and-control regulation,
31–33, 39
conclusions, 38–41
consequences of overcriminalization
trend, 27–38
criticism, 38–41
damage to moral fabric of culture
and, 36–37
diminished constitutional protections,
14, 26–27
diminished role of intent, 14, 18–25,
40–41
dispute resolution, 40
economic effects, 28–33
examples of overcriminalization
trends, 11–13
greater intrusiveness, 14, 25–26
impulse to punish, 9–11
increased complexity and, 14–18,
20–26
moral impacts, 33–38
overuse, 36–37
problems of application, 14–27
reserved for flagrant/repetitive
violations, 64
resource requirements, 29–31, 41
EPA. See Environmental Protection
Agency (EPA)
Evidence
EPAs use of "indirect estimates" as,
27
lowered credible evidence standards,
14
rules of evidence, 27, 129–30, 150
Ex post facto clause, 48

Fahey, Helen, 95, 110
Fair notice, 20–21, 40
False Claims Act, 10
Farmers, ranchers, and hunters

Fourth Amendment protections, 55
MBTA and, 58
FBI. See Federal Bureau of Investigation
(FBI), Environmental Crimes Unit
Fear of Judging, 132
Federal budget, 36
Project Exile Act, 96
Project Safe Neighborhood funding,
103–4
Federal Bureau of Investigation (FBI),
Environmental Crimes Unit, 55
Federal courts
advantages for firearms cases, 95
clogging, xiv, 102–3
Federal Courts Study Committee, 120
Federal crimes, number of, vii, 4, 99
Federal jail sentences, location of
incarceration, 95, 110–11
Federalism, 96–99, 112–14
Project Safe Neighborhood's frontal
assault on, 99–105
"respect for federalism," 93–94,
96–97, 100, 104–5, 113–14
Federalization of crime, xiv, 98–99
consequences, 102–10
political justification, 112–13
See also Project Exile; Project Safe
Neighborhoods
Fifth Amendment protections
double jeopardy and dual
sovereignty and, xiii, 27, 45, 59–61,
65
due process, 47, 48–49, 108
prosecutorial immunity and, 63–64,
65
regulatory exception and, xiii, 27,
48–52
self-incrimination, xiii, 14, 27, 45,
62–64, 65
undermining, xii
Firearm offenses. See Project Exile;
Project Safe Neighborhoods
Firearm regulations, 53
"prohibited-person-in-possession"
statute, 106–7
Florida, 2
Mills prosecution, 22–23
Ford, Brian I., 107
Forfeiture of property, 10, 37
Fourteenth Amendment, 47, 108
Fourth Amendment protections, xii,
xiii, 45
warrant requirement, xiii, 27, 52–56,
64

Cato Institute

Founded in 1977, the Cato Institute is a public policy research foundation dedicated to broadening the parameters of policy debate to allow consideration of more options that are consistent with the traditional American principles of limited government, individual liberty, and peace. To that end, the Institute strives to achieve greater involvement of the intelligent, concerned lay public in questions of policy and the proper role of government.

The Institute is named for *Cato's Letters*, libertarian pamphlets that were widely read in the American Colonies in the early 18th century and played a major role in laying the philosophical foundation for the American Revolution.

Despite the achievement of the nation's Founders, today virtually no aspect of life is free from government encroachment. A pervasive intolerance for individual rights is shown by government's arbitrary intrusions into private economic transactions and its disregard for civil liberties.

To counter that trend, the Cato Institute undertakes an extensive publications program that addresses the complete spectrum of policy issues. Books, monographs, and shorter studies are commissioned to examine the federal budget, Social Security, regulation, military spending, international trade, and myriad other issues. Major policy conferences are held throughout the year, from which papers are published thrice yearly in the *Cato Journal*. The Institute also publishes the quarterly magazine *Regulation*.

In order to maintain its independence, the Cato Institute accepts no government funding. Contributions are received from foundations, corporations, and individuals, and other revenue is generated from the sale of publications. The Institute is a nonprofit, tax-exempt, educational foundation under Section 501(c)3 of the Internal Revenue Code.

CATO INSTITUTE
1000 Massachusetts Ave., N.W.
Washington, D.C. 20001
www.cato.org